SEPT. '39

by

Robert C. Vansword

SEPT.'39

Robert C. Vansword

ESPress, Inc.
Washington, D.C. 20011

I.S.B.N. 0-917200-22-5

CONTENTS

ILLUSTRATIONS

The author,
Robert C. Vansword
in a 1939 photograph.

Robert C. Vansword today.

DEDICATION

To the simple Polish farmers who fell, who disappeared without a trace, who became prisoners of war, who died in prisons and hell camps, who carried on the fight abroad or in the underground—to these simple, modest Polish men and women and to their mothers who brought them up, is this work dedicated.

PREFACE

In the midst of the hardest and bloodiest fighting between the Germans and the Poles in September, 1939, the Soviet Army without warning or a declaration of war crossed the eastern border of Poland on the 17th day of September and attacked the Poles from the rear. This resulted in a complete annihilation of the Polish armed forces. There was no way for the Poles to resist simultaneously Germany and Soviet Russia, whose combined population of more than a quarter of a billion people produced incredibly high odds against Poland: 1:10.5 in men; 1:35 in armoured vehicles; 1:62 in fighter airplanes; 1:52 in navy tonnage. These odds were made possible only by the war preparedness of those countries at the expense of hundreds of billions of marks and rubles, respectively.

The Hitler-Stalin friendship agreement concluded in August, 1939 in a secret clause provided for the partition of Poland along the Bug and San Rivers, but numerous German forces crossed this line and were attacking the Poles east of it. They bypassed many Polish units and left them practically untouched. A *few* Polish units were dispersed without being annihilated, while some others attempted to reach Rumania and Hungary. The Germans pushed eastward until they came in contact with the Soviet forces that were advancing westward. Upon their meeting, the Germans had to make an about face and retreat to the Bug-San line as previously agreed to by the secret clause of the Ribbentrop-Molotov pact. The distance between the retreating Germans and the advancing Russians was set for 15 to 20 kilometers in order to avoid any possible incidents between those newly created allies. The Russo-German border line running along the Bug-San Rivers became established on or around the 27th of September.

Because the promised assistance of France and England did not materialize, the last large pockets of the Polish resistance had to capitulate: Warsaw—on September 27; Modlin—on September 29; Pomeranian Hel—on October 2; the army of General Kleeberg—on October 5. Thus, the German propaganda by Goebbels was a pack of lies when it announced to the world that Poland had fallen during a two-week "blitz".

The Polish soldiers who were not taken prisoners attempted to don civilian clothing and either reach their homes or cross the borders of Rumania and Hungary. Thus there was a constant movement on all roads, highways, and even forest paths, crowded not only by former soldiers, but especially by the civilian population dislocated from their homes and escaping the oncoming Germans, planning to return when hostilities ceased. The human traffic occurred in all imaginable directions, but followed the east-west route more than the north-south. Generally, shortcuts were used by all and the main highways were avoided because of the devastation as well as check and control points set by the occupants along the main communication arteries. Thus ended the month of September, 1939.

It is of utmost interest, however, to know about the details of the beginning acts of the war. One of them is of striking importance. It concerns the pretext that Hitler had to invent for international opinion as an excuse for attacking Poland on September 1. William L. Shirer describes it vividly and in detail in his "Rise and Fall of the Third Reich" (soft cover edition, sixth Crest printing, 1964, pages 691 - 694 and 788 - 789). The Fuhrer's invention was simple and effective. In order to convince the world that it was the Poles who attacked first and crossed the border into Germany, Hitler's plan called for a dozen Germans masquerading as Polish soldiers to attack the radio station in Gleiwitz, kill the radio station personnel, deliver a short German-abusive speech in the Polish language declaring that the Polish army had begun to march against Germany and destroy the radio station. The hoax was perpetrated with attention to the smallest detail. Thirteen German criminals were drugged, put in Polish army uniforms, which were provided by Admiral Canaris, head of the German army counter-intelligence, and killed by the SS men at the radio station. Upon accomplishment of their mission those SS men were "put out of the way" according to a Nuremberg witness, General Lahousen of the German counter-intelligence. The photographs of the dead "Polish" soldiers were made by the correspondents of the most influential western world newspapers including the *New York Times*. The articles which appeared in the world press on September 1, 1939, without exception ascribed the guilt to the Poles, who in reality were entirely innocent but now were declared guilty by international opinion. Thus the unsuspecting American press, publicly duped by the Nazi gangsters, blamed Poland and excused Hitler for "carrying the war back into the Polish territories." The German propaganda was once more able to convince the West that the Poles provoked Hitler by the Gleiwitz incident and that the "innocent, patient Third Reich" only defended itself against the Polish blood-thirsty armed mob. The truth was not revealed until the 1946 Nuremberg trial of the German criminals of war. Until that time the Poles were considered culprits. The Gleiwitz affair was not an isolated case. During the night of August 31/September 1, 1939, numerous SS men performed identical attacks in German localities near the Polish border, including the same scenario with dead men in Polish uniforms. The dead men left behind them appeared to be Polish soldiers. It was Gleiwitz, however, which was the largest stage set with the spectacular execution of the fantastically nefarious plans of Hitler.

It was actually August, 1939, which was the month of incessant incidents fabricated by the Germans. The purpose was to show the world "Polish atrocities" and to provoke the Poles. But the Poles had to keep quiet whether they wanted to or not. The French and English journalists, politicians, and other observers cruised on the Polish side of the German border watching, pleading, then threatening the Polish authorities to refrain from reacting to the Nazi provocation, to keep cool, because their respective governments would not stand for the Poles firing the first shot. France and England—especially France—pleaded with the Polish government not to mobilize her forces and not to provoke Germany—the latter having been completely mobilized and prepared for the war. The Polish government accommodated its allies and did not order a total mobilization. Poland was attacked on September 1, without having mobilized all of her forces. Fortunately, a partial call to arms was quietly carried out. Thus it is August, 1939 which deserves special attention as the most important month for the unfolding of the hypocrisy of German lawlessness along the Polish border toward the almost half-a-million Polish minority in Germany, in the free city of Gdansk (in German,Danzig) and the work of the German saboteurs and fifth columnists in Poland.

The German fifth column in Poland consisted not only of Germans, but unfortunately also of Ukrainians who were Polish citizens. The Germans took advantage of the animosity between the Poles and the Ukrainians which had endured for four centuries. This condition had come to a peak on November 1, 1918, when the Ukrainian nationalists proclaimed an independent Ukrainian State in the territories east of the San River. These territories had been continually contested by Poland and the princedoms of Rus.

The events of November, 1918 resulted in bloodshed. The Ukrainians attacked the unsuspecting Poles, who immediately organized and resisted their attackers. Atrocities were perpetrated by both sides upon their own enemies who in many instances were inhumanly tortured and then murdered. This war lasted for about a year. The two warring sides arrived at a decision to liberate the Kiev Ukraine. They then formed an alliance directed against the Soviets and occupied the right shore of the Dnieper River, including Kiev. The Soviet armies then counter-attacked and pushed back the combined Polish-Ukrainian forces near Warsaw, where in turn the Poles launched another offensive and put the Soviet armies into retreat. In 1921 a peace treaty was signed by Poland and Soviet Russia, over the vehement disagreement of the Ukrainians, who argued that the war should be continued. The Poles were exhausted not only by the war against the Soviets, but also by German attacks upon their rear in Silesia and from the Czechs, who captured Teschen, Silesia. Thus Poland had to fight on three fronts. In order not to lose her newly resurrected State and liberty, then only two years of age, it was necessary for Poland to conclude peace with the Soviets. At this point the Germans began to woo the Polish Ukrainians, promising them an independent Ukrainian State as a reward for their unconditional cooperation with Germany.

After 1933, when Hitler became master of Germany, the Ukrainians were instructed to help in the destruction of the Polish State. Many of their youths were sent clandestinely to Germany from Poland in order to attend courses in espionage, sabotage, fifth column techniques and psychological warfare. Upon their return to Poland they organized underground activities in their communities. They received arms and ammunition from Germany, as well as the newest political directives. Many were active in the Organization of Ukrainian Nationalists, known by its three initials, O.U.N. In August, 1939 they received explicit orders from Germany to act against the Polish war effort, and were notified about the impending German attack on Poland. Their reply to their German masters was that they were ready and that they awaited with impatience the beginning of the war.

The Byelorussian national minority in Poland had been most loyal throughout the course of Polish history and it remained so during the six long years of the war. In contrast to the Germans and Ukrainians, who lived on hospitable Polish soil, simultaneously preparing treason and bloodshed against it, the Byelorussians stood out as exemplary liberty and freedom fighters battling side by side with the Polish neighbors and brothers against the forces of evil and darkness.

The situation of the Jews in Poland in the years immediately preceding the Second World War deserves special attention. Upon the incorporation of Austria into Hitler's Reich in 1938, close to 200,000 Jews escaped to Czechoslovakia and Poland. Many of them came to Austria from Germany, where organized persecution had been raging since 1933. Despite having a Jewish population of over three million, Poland opened her doors to the refugees in the best Polish tradition, dating back to the tenth century. With the dismemberment of Czechoslovakia by Hitler in the spring of 1939, the Czechoslovakian Jews, as well as those who had come there from Austria and Germany, fled to Poland. There was also a constant flow of Jews to Poland directly from Germany or indirectly through Hungary, Rumania, France, Denmark, the Baltic and Scandinavian countries and Gdansk. Poland received them all, regardless of the fact that she was herself overpopulated and that the Poles themselves were emigrating to France, Germany and America.

It is to Poland's highest credit that hundreds of thousands of Jews found shelter there. It was Poland who conceived the pre-war plan for settling the Jews in Israel (then named Palestine) in cooperation with England and France. The suggestion was rejected by those countries and Poland was vilified as anti-Semitic. Had the Polish plan been accepted, the wholesale slaughter of the Jews by the Nazis during the Second World War would not have occurred. On the contrary, all—I repeat—all the Jews would have been saved from death. The immense tragedy could have been averted.

Some Jews were able to emigrate from Poland just before the outbreak of war in September, 1939 and for them Poland had provided the precious time to save their lives. Refugee centers were set up in every large Polish city, and the Polish Red Cross, together with other organizations, cared for women and children as the first priority and attempted to provide the men with employment. Many women were widowed and many children orphaned and destitute after having lost all their possessions during their escape from the Nazi murderers.

Until the last days before September 1939, more and more Jewish refugees continued to arrive in Poland. They came in small groups by air, car and railroad, and in larger groups by ship through the ports of Gdynia and Gdansk (Danzig). Many crossed the German-Polish border illegally.

It was in August that the German takeover of the Free City of Danzig (Gdansk) was plotted with the assistance of 168 German army officers, sent there for that express purpose. The Germans had smuggled in a large supply of arms and ammunition, among them twelve light and four heavy artillery pieces. Western Poland was inundated by German arms and ammunition smuggled in by German consuls Moeldecke and Damerau, by car under diplomatic immunity, and by the German senators (in the senate of Poland) Wiesner and Wambeck. German fifth columnists bombed German schools and churches in Poland and Nazi propaganda screamed that it was the Poles. The western press obligingly repeated the German lies.

To this August prelude, September, 1939 came as an epilogue. September marked the height of the heroism of the Polish soldier, who, deprived of sleep and food, had to fight during the day and march during the night. Twenty-four hours a day for weeks—three, four, five—he fought against the superior arms of the adversary against the highest odds in the history of mankind, under enemy controlled skies filled with incessant strafing and bombing aircraft. The soldier, hopelessly outnumbered. was hit not only from the air, but also on the ground by devastatingly superior weapons. This typical Polish soldier was no sophisticated city dweller, for almost 80 percent of the soldiers were small farmers. This young Polish farm boy, accustomed to his peaceful little village and the soft sounds of friendly animals, had to suffer the roar of aerial bombs, grenades, heavy artillery, the smoke of his burning countryside and the horrible smell of rotting human and animal flesh. He had to fight knowing that his whole country was seized by the enemy. He fought...and he was often victorious. Even after his whole country fell into the hands of the Germans and Russians, he refused to disband but carried on quick-moving partisan warfare, or crossed over to Rumania and Hungary and thence to the Near East, France, and England...continuing his struggle for Polish liberty by fighting for all freedom loving people.

xix

WE GO TO WAR

The Polish summer of 1939 was anything but quiet. After the annexation of Austria and the Czechs, Slovakia was made Hitler's vassal state and the German pincers encircled Poland from the north (East Prussia), west (Germany), and south (Slovakia).

It was obvious even to us, the 17 year olds, that Poland was next on Germany's list. But we could not believe that Hitler would attack, for we had faith in the military agreements between Poland, England and France which called for war on Germany if she should attack Poland. We were certain that the Polish armed forces were well prepared for war. The young Polish Air Force was the special object of our admiration. In 1935 and 1937, international aviation shows known as "Challenges" were won by the Poles, confirming our opinion that Polish aircraft and pilots were the best. Patriotic feeling ran high and even the man in the street, whose lot was far from good in our country (Poland was ravaged from 1914 - 1921 by the armies of Austria-Germany, Tsarist Russia, and the Bolshevik Soviet Union), was offering his last valuables to the national defense fund. The people were not rich, for their country received no Western financial assistance after the First World War, but they were proud. They believed that their cause was good and that God was on their side.

On August 28, late in the evening, I returned from pilot training, which I had completed with much greater ease than I had anticipated. After a hot bath and a cup of hot chocolate served to me in bed by my mother, I dared for the first time in my life to smoke a cigarette in her presence. She just smiled faintly. But it was destined that I should not sleep that night. Still smoking my cherished cigarette, which in my mind had grown into a symbol of my manhood and maturity, I heard a knock at the door. A soldier walked in. In his outstretched hand he held a piece of paper.

"Are you Robert C. Vansword, sir?"

"Yes. That's me."

"Please accept this and sign the receipt."

I did as I was asked. He thanked me, saluted and left. Mother started to cry. She knew what it was. The mobilization order assigned me to military auxiliary duties as a liaison cadet - officer between the regimental and corps command headquarters.

I was to report at once. I dressed in a hurry. Still crying, but without a word, mother slipped a large denomination bill into my pocket. I left on my bicycle and ten minutes later reported to the officer on duty at the regimental headquarters.

I was not alone. Many of my classmates were there awaiting orders. After a wait we were told to report for 12-hour duty the next day and sent home.

It is difficult to describe our elation at being mobilized. We were happy to be needed and wanted to serve our country to the last breath. After all, we stood on the side of justice, righteousness, and gentility. For us to prevail was only a question of time, but we still hoped for peace and took the "whole show" as just a probe of strength. Doubts were simply non-existent. Our country was protected by treaties: with the Soviets it was a mutual non-aggression pact and we had an identical pact with Nazi Germany, as well as friendship agreements with France and England.

It was France, the victor during the 1914-1918 war, in whom we believed. France was an ideal of democracy, political wisdom, valor, heroism and military know-how. In a word, she appeared invincible.

And England! Not as vivacious as France, but cool and considerate, "queen of the seas." Perfectly organized and "without emotions." We had some reservations about the behavior of Messrs. Daladier and Chamberlain a year earlier in Munich when they capitulated before Hitler, but we excused this on the grounds that it was the Czech army which did not want to fight. And indeed, the lack of fighting spirit in the Czech nation had been well observed since the end of the Medieval Ages.

We knew that Hitler must be defeated and were readying ourselves to contribute to his downfall in the speediest imaginable way. Of course, being well read about the situation in Europe, we trusted in the indomitable spirit of freedom always present within Western civilization. It is good to be seventeen and have high ideals!

From headquarters we walked slowly toward the downtown section of the city. I walked alongside my

bike with my friend Zbig. He didn't have one. We philo-
sophized about the war, peace and life in general. I had
met him for the first time when I was thirteen and our
friendship had grown through the years. I lost my father
when I was twelve. Zbig's father was always traveling
and my friend seldom saw him. We were in similar,
though different situations, and we communicated easily.
Before saying "so-long" that early morning we resolved
not to separate during the whole warlike period.

There were not many hours between our parting
that night and seeing each other again on the next day.
As agreed, we kept close to each other every passing day,
becoming practically inseparable without any special
effort on our part. Zbig's easy conversation, well-
developed sense of humor, a certain mild cynicism under
which mask he preferred to hide stronger emotions, his
humanistic love of the underdog—all those characteristics
caused me to like him more each hour that we spent together, and the hours were many.

Our service involved basic duties of liaison personnel accompanying the "brass" to various local headquarters and bringing them back to the airport or to their
cars. We delivered many top secret documents, letters,
plans, maps, charts, etc. from one command to another.
When alone, we used our bikes. Sometimes for more
urgent assignments, it was motorcycles of the motor pool
or even cars, each vehicle having the service of an NCO
army chauffeur.

The last days of August were splendid. The sun was
warm and we were in the midst of a wonderful Polish
Indian summer. The international news, however, was

less beautiful. Germany signed a political agreement with the Soviets and we were afraid that Poland would suffer.

The night of August 31 found us both on duty. It was not a busy night and we dozed off on the soft easy chairs in the same large lounge which had served us before. We were awakened suddenly and rudely by the guards, who informed us of the early morning German attack on Poland. We smiled happily. With the Officer of the Day's wine, we drank a toast to our victory. Some older officers behaved more seriously. And we knew why, for in our hears we felt an almost imperceptible pressure which made them beat faster, and our throats became tighter at flashing thoughts about our immediate future. Contacting our commanding officer at once, we volunteered for front line duty immediately. He flatly refused, saying that we were urgently needed at the Army Corps Headquarters. We did not argue, but saluted and left his office. Just outside the door we stopped as if on command and looked at each other. We smiled simultaneously — and we understood each other.

"Let's not lose time here while the Front needs us," said Zbig. Instead of an answer I gave him a broad smile.

Our city was bombed during the late hours of the morning. Damages were inflicted on the airport, but no airplanes were lost. The downtown section had some casualties.

The same afternoon, just after duty hours, we began modest preparations to depart. Our mothers had to be left in complete darkness; we knew that for their own good they had to be spared the knowledge of our departure. Leaving our homes in secrecy, like thieves, no matter how high our motives, contributed to our feeling of guilt. We didn't want to face our parents' tears and their certain disapproval. I got together all I needed: two changes of underwear, a few pairs of socks, a warm sweater, and a flannel shirt.

The next question was how to provide some food for Mother and my younger brother, for all stores were bursting with people who wanted to buy supplies for the hard days to come. The next day I went to a large flour mill in the suburbs and purchased 200 pounds of flour which I brought home.

Mother was working as an emergency nurse in the military hospital, for she too volunteered her services. Many wounded soldiers and civilians were transported from the front lines to our hospital and Mother was quite busy. This enabled me to keep the preparations for my departure secret from her.

September 3 was Sunday. The news from the western Polish borders was not encouraging. The German armored forces were advancing rapidly, breaking up valiant Polish resistance. I went to church, but instead of praying I was thinking constantly: "When shall we leave? How can we join a military formation departing in the Western direction?" I was not yet 18 years of age and this was the greatest handicap for me, because every unit commander turned me away as soon as he found out that I was below the military age! We made our plans and decided not to show any documents. We would have to lie and say that we lost them. Our statements had to sound credible. We would have to keep straight faces and steady eyes when the crucial moment came.

WE GO TO WAR

September 4—Monday. All preparations were finished. Our few belongings were packed in two small suitcases. Tomorrow we would leave. More wounded were filling our hospitals and masses of civilians were fleeing eastward in order not to be taken by the Germans. Our city was bombed again and a few were killed. We didn't actually see anything for we were on duty at the headquarters in the suburbs. We only heard German planes dropping bombs. The air attack was short, perhaps seven or eight minutes. Where was our fine air force? Probably busy at the front lines—but we didn't like it.

September 5—Tuesday. We didn't report to duty at 8:00 AM as assigned. How could we, when at 7:00 AM we were already at the main railroad station casting about for a train departing West. We decided not to board a military train before it started to move, for if the train were still stationary, the military authorities would have time enough after checking us out to simply order us off. But we knew full well that no one would push us out of a train in motion. In the uniforms of the Officer-Cadet College we would simply force our presence upon the train commander and convince him of our value to his unit.

There were a dozen trains waiting for departure. We got into the first one which began to move. It was a train with cars designed before the war for transportation of goods and merchandise. Now the transported wares were soldiers. We jumped nimbly on the steps of the nearest coach and soldiers standing in the widely opened doors pulled us in.

"Where is the train commander?" I shouted.

"In the back coach, in the back!"

"Thanks!" We jumped off. The train was still moving very slowly. We ran toward the back.

"Where is the train commander?" we kept shouting at the cars which we were passing. Finally we heard:

"In the next coach, in the next coach!"

The train was still not moving too fast. We jumped in. There were tables standing near two opened doors. A few officers sat at them, leaning over some papers. We saluted. As previously agreed, I was the first to address the highest ranking officer—a major.

"Major, sir! Air Force Cadet Officer Vansword reports his arrival and asks to be admitted into the ranks!" Zbig recited the same "sacred" formula.

We stood at rigid attention with serious faces, our eyes pleading. The major gave us a long quizzical look as he stood up and returned the military salute.

"A good sign," I thought, and I was certain that Zbig must have thought the same. Two other officers, a captain and a lieutenant, who were seated at the same table, also stood up and saluted us back.

"That's good" flashed through my head.

The whole scene took maybe ten seconds.

"Where are you from?" asked the major. The tone of his voice was harsh, but not unfriendly. His eyes— hurrah!—betrayed him. There was a faint trace of a smile in them. Feeling reassured, I replied:

"We are both from here, from Lvov. To the present time we have not been assigned permanently to any unit," I lied, "and we have been told to keep in readiness for any

8

forthcoming orders which have not come, while the front lines need us and we can be of use on the front lines.''

The major's face became less set. A one-tenth-of-a second glance at the faces of his two younger colleagues convinced me that we were making progress with them also. The first lieutenant especially impressed me with an almost open smile on his friendly face.

"Your documents!" The major extended his hand.

"We have lost them! But I am almost 19." I was adding more than one full year to my age and praying for success. "With your permission I can submit the proof for my words by telephoning to the city authorities at the next train stop." Here I bent the truth boldly, for we all knew that a long distance telephone call was next to impossible. Five days of war had inflicted much damage on the cities and destroyed many telephone lines. Our eyes were concentrated with force and determination on the major's face. There was a long pause.

"Well!" he said deliberately, "you are accepted temporarily." I felt sure that he himself didn't know the precise meaning of the word "temporarily." And he continued:

"And only on a trial basis." Again I thought that he knew fairly well that the word "trial" was a mere formality uttered just for the sake of appearances and military orderliness.

"You will report at the next train stop to the sergeant-major, the quartermaster of the battalion, who will register and assign you according to the regulations and provide you with rations! Have you had breakfast?"

"No, Major, sir! Yes, Major, sir! Just coffee! We had coffee! We didn't have time for more!"

"All right. Report also to the kitchen for a solid breakfast!"

"Yes, Major, sir. Thank you, Major, sir!"

We were accepted into the army.

THE ARMY TRAIN

The train rolled slowly west towards the front. There were many trains loaded to full capacity with refugees, men, women, old, young, children and babies, and all the goods of the families, but those trains were going east, deeper into Poland, away from the German attackers. Our train stopped frequently opposite the refugee trains. It was hard to believe our eyes. Alarm, noise, crying babies and children, wailing mothers, men asking a thousand questions, nervous, unshaven, dirty... Those were people gripped by panic, by fear of the Germans, the people who looked for peaceful surroundings to await the end of the war just begun. Families torn asunder, many separated men in the armed forces, women with children and older folks awaiting the arrival of the train at a city, at any city where there was peace, where they could eat something warm, where they could wash themselves and their children and tend to the bare necessities of life in unfamiliar places. Worst of all, many people had been under fire or bombing by the Germans; family members were crazed after the loss of a child, baby or children. Some had temporary bandaged wounds with patches of blood soaking through the bandages and caked dark red. Some of their stories were hair-raising, some were incoherent, stuttering, repeating the word "dead, dead" without end. We looked, listened and our hearts and souls—as well as our food—went out to them. But some of the soldiers were becoming numb. In their passivity or introverted state, some men didn't give anything, as if afraid that their food would be insufficient for themselves.

This was my first encounter with basic animalistic greed and egocentrism—with the complete or partial lack of spirit to assist a brother or sister—or open hesitation to help—or simple shock at the other man's suffering.

Those were sights which did nothing to encourage the soldier going to war. Every one of us who asked himself the question, "Could this happen to my family?" must have answered with a "no," an illogical "no," an egotistical "no," with a hopeful "no"—because I am the center of the universe and nothing like that could ever happen to me, to ME!

Perhaps not all, not each and every soldier, thought these thoughts, but most faces were set in sadness and comprehension.

We were glad when our train started to roll again, but nothing could eradicate those sights from our eyes, or those shouts from our ears, and nothing could make us forget.

Other trains of refugees were luckier. The people had had time to prepare for evacuation; they were not touched by the horrors of war—they did not know. Many a young girl sent us a happy inviting smile that was left unanswered—but not always, for sometimes a young, carefree devil was able to shout back something more or less complimentary. The eternal woman! Life tried to assert itself amidst chaos and death.

THE ARMY TRAIN

The train was passing through countryside unscathed by the war. Young boys and girls with baskets full of red apples, yellow pears or bluish plums, threw ripe fruit to us. There were not many misses, for the train rolled slowly over freshly repaired tracks which had been damaged by aerial bombing, or over temporarily repaired bridges and road crossings. The smiles of the girls, the joyful shouts of the young boys, their fresh village faces remained in our memories, but even they could not make us forget. . .

The dog is really superior to the human being in his ability to forget the bad and in his eternal joy after no matter how great a sorrow. Man, on the contrary, forgets joys easily, but remembers unhappiness unto eternity. And he too rarely forgives!

The first day to travel took us 150 kilometers, a miraculous distance for the train, considering the bombed stations, the damaged bridges and rails and especially the almost incessant bombings to which we were exposed. On the average of once every two hours the German planes flew over us, some dropping bombs, and others machine-gunning us. As soon as they were spotted, the train stopped and everybody dispersed rapidly. Our heavy anti-aircraft machine guns placed in a hurry started to bark immediately, but we didn't have enough of them. Fortunately for us, the train did not seem to be rated by the Germans as a primary target. Their bombers appeared reluctant to drop their loads on us—as if they had some more important target—a fact which did not make us unhappy. Some of their formations flew over us at altitudes that could not be reached by our machine guns, which nevertheless blasted at them with no visible effect.

The night was spent in the coaches. We were warm and well fed. Tired, we fell asleep quickly and slept until dawn. In the morning we heard that by late afternoon or early evening we would arrive at our destination. Zbig and I looked at each other questioningly, for we had been sure that this unit would be unloaded at the very front lines. We were somewhat east of Rzeszow. How was it that the Germans were so close?

From Rzeszow the train was directed south toward the city of Jaslo. At about 5:00 PM, without reaching that city, our unit received orders to unload. At a small railroad station we contacted some civilians and railroad officials, who told us that the Germans were as far as 60 kilometers west of us. Zbig and I had no intention of waiting here for them and decided to leave the military unit, to travel further west to the front lines, where it would be very easy to join a combat unit. Our empty train began pulling out toward the southwest and the city of Jaslo. We boarded it and half an hour later arrived at that city's railroad station. And here we were thunderstruck upon being notified by military officials that there was no transportation whatsoever toward the west. We were crushed by this news. We could not reach the front! Worse, there were no military units in the immediate vicinity. All of them were already deployed either west or eastward from us.

"What shall we do?" asked Zbig.

"Hm...We are in a fix. The only two directions open

are due east in the direction of Dobromil or back north—
where we just came from!"

"Shall we rejoin the unit we just left?"

"We can, but wouldn't you feel funny?"

"Yes, I would feel ashamed. How about you?"

"Me too!"

"Well! Let's go east! Maybe we can find some other
unit!"

"Fine! Let's do it!"

We asked about trains departing toward the east.
There was one leaving soon and we boarded it at once. It
was one of those trains for evacuated civilians. The
majority of them were young men of military age who
hoped to be outfitted and armed in the eastern Polish
territories. Their mood was pensive and we understood it,
for the German advance was too rapid even for an opti-
mist. Our general conversation, however, was not
gloomy, because we all knew that nothing was lost yet.
We knew that our faithful Western allies, England and
France, would never forsake us; moreover, there was
confirmed news that the English fleet had entered the
Baltic and that landings had been made near Gdansk,
while the French army had entered Rumania. We preferred not to voice any doubt at these reports—which
later proved to be rumors—because we were not certain
about them ourselves.

Night was falling quickly. Our train moved slowly,
stopped frequently, and made little headway. It was
morning before it brought us to the little town of Chyrov.
We were hungry, sleepy and tired.

"What now?" asked Zbig.

"Well, let's go among the trains, maybe we will find what we are looking for!"

"Aren't you hungry?"

"Yes. And you?"

"Of course. But where can we get food?"

"We could go to a distribution center for the evacuated, but we are soldiers, aren't we?"

"Well, we could always do that, if we do not join a military unit."

"So. Let's look for one."

We walked toward that part of the railroad station which was designed for the loading and unloading of freight trains. Some trains were standing idle and empty. In one we saw an artillery unit and didn't like it; another was unloading an infantry formation. We kept walking across the rails, ducking under coaches.

"Do you see what I see?" I asked.

"Yes! Beautiful!"

And indeed, they were beautiful: grey, chestnut, black, white, brown, beige—splendid and patient thorou-breds looking at us with their big innocent eyes. Their bodies, lean and strong, were shining in the rays of the morning sun. I looked at Zbig and I saw him smile. I smiled, too.

"How shall we get in?"

"Exactly as we did two days ago!"

"Will it work this time?"

"It did the first time we tried!"

"Let's try it, then!"

The train in which the cavalry unit was being transported must have arrived at the station the evening before. The soldiers were just now beginning to stir and get up. We asked the guards for the whereabouts of the commanding officer, went straight to his quarters at the middle of the train, and reported to him dutifully.

The impression we made upon the captain commanding the squadron must have been good, for we were accepted "on trial."

The squadron's staff sergeant, Zhichi, was to be our supervisor. We were supposed to keep close to him and to assist him. In the late morning, after breakfast, which we devoured greedily, the train was again on the move. But after an hour it stopped and the order to unload was given. We did our best to be helpful and we noted that our efforts were appreciated. From the railroad station the column trotted west; we remained with the supply train, i.e., the horse-drawn carts full of ammunition, food for men and horses, spare parts for carts, harnesses, etc. Our orders were to ride on two different carts and to assist the drivers. We could not show our discontentment with such an easy and, in our opinion, undignified assignment. To a certain extent we were right in our indignation, for we knew that not too far to the west men were fighting and dying in defence of the nation, and we—we were helping to drive horse carts with food for horses! Hell, we didn't feel too great.

The cart train had to join up with the quartered squadron that night, to supply the men and horses, and the next evening, to join the squadron again in order to repeat its vital but nevertheless boring function. We wanted to fight, but instead here we were driving a cart on the mountain roads, forest paths, and often over the roadless fields and hills. Some of the going was rough. The cold of the mountains was getting to us. We had neither warm coats nor blankets. The night was dark and chilly. I tried to sleep between sacks full of horse fodder, but no luck. The sacks were constantly shifting due to the steep rises and drops in the roads and ground covered with exposed tree stumps, heavy roots, and stones. From time to time the carts ahead stopped and ours had to stop too. The noise of the carts and horses, the shouts of men, commands, all were anything but conducive to sleeping. Close to daylight, we arrived at our destination, just in time to start supplying the squadron. Sunrise came and brought some warmth with it. I waited impatiently for an opportunity to sleep or just to doze off, and even a warm, hearty army breakfast did not restore my energy. Finally around noon I was able to sleep some, and afterwards I felt great again, as if I had slept the whole night.

We were in the Carpathians, about 20 kilometers west of Dobromil, and our orders were to proceed north toward Neezhauk, but, what a surprise! Shortly before the carts were to move the captain came to us. We saluted.

"Do you know how to read maps?" he asked.

"Yes, Captain, sir!" we answered in unison.

"Very good! We have two motorcycles and two chauffeurs. You are going to be responsible for keeping perfect liaison between divisional command and the squadron commander, which is me. You are to direct the chauffeurs and to find the divisional command posts, which will be located in a different place each day. Are you prepared to assume this responsibility?"

"Yes, Captain, sir!"

He saluted us and we hastened to return his salute, which was saying without words that we ought to go on.

In no time we found the motorcycles and the chauffeurs, who already had orders for us. Within two minutes we were speeding toward the place indicated as the divisional command post.

We were happy. We felt needed and we knew that we were contributing to the all-powerful effort of the nation to crush the enemy.

The Falcon [Sokol] 600, with side-car, a predecessor of the model #1000 used by the author during early battle action in 1939.

FALCON 1000

The Falcon motorcycle first found the light of day in 1939 in the Central Automotive Works in Warsaw, and it was a beautiful Polish motorcycle, admired without exception by the whole command of the 38th Infantry Reserve Division, which the Falcon henceforth was to serve. The sheet steel of its fenders shone with dark camouflage green, contrasting sharply with the outer parts of the motor, oxidized and tarnished black. There was a small hand machine gun attached to the top of the side car.

By fate's decision it went to war straight from the factory with a motor still not broken in, and with virginal looking shining new tires which had not yet felt the asphalt streets of the capital, the hard stone laid surface of the state highways, the dust of side roads, or the pot holes and roots of forest paths.

The divisional command parted with the Falcon with a heavy heart, but it was expedient to assign it to the cavalry squadron to provide the fastest means of personal communication. I received the Falcon together with a sergeant-chauffeur, Vladislav Koval, with whom I immediately drank a "bruderschaft." Not only did I like him at first glance, but I also had to have him "on my side." Vlad was a young, polite and energetic soldier, who had graduated with distinction only the year before from the professional military school for NCO's. I noted with satisfaction that he accepted me immediately as his superior.

From the very moment I received the Falcon I fell in love with it. It was the love at first sight which a soldier feels for his weapon—which becomes his shield, defense, friend and protector. Even that early in my life I was of the opinion that the so-called "inanimate objects" which we úse should be liked and cherished by their possessors. It seemed logical and clear to me that any object we like, we keep in the best possible shape, giving it the finest care and attention. A part of our personality, no matter how small, becomes involved in that object and it is then that such objects take on for some people, certain personalized dimensions. Consider the case with a car. Is it not constructed in the image of man? People compare the head of a man with the hood; the eyes became lights; the nose is the top of the hood; the mouth—the front of the radiator; the ears—the side mirrors; the vocal cords—the horn; the body—remains the body; the hands and feet—four wheels; the arms and legs—the wheel suspension; the nerves—the electrical system; the digestive system—the oil lines; the stomach—the gas tank; the derriere—the rear end. This comparison struck me in a coherent and funny way the first time I became aware of it. Now, I see in every vehicle the combination of "dead" matter with "living" aspects—and this was my perception of the Falcon motorcycle, even though it was quite different from an automobile.

A few minutes after having received the motorcycle I was summoned to Squadron headquarters where I was handed an open envelope with an official message. The aide-de-camp instructed me with the following words:

"The command post of the division is located in the village of Boratyn about thirty-four kilometers from our present position toward the north-northeast. Please take this report to the divisional commander. In ten minutes you will learn the content of the message by heart, word for word, and then you will report to me to check your memory."

"Yes lieutenant, sir," I answered smartly.

Four minutes later I knew the message by heart to the complete satisfaction of the officer. Within the next minute we were on our way to the division command post, riding as fast as the narrow forest road permitted. The open map showed me the way perfectly.

"Turn right onto the highway at the next intersection!" I shouted to the chauffeur, trying to be heard over the motor and the rushing airstream.

He heard me all right, nodded his head in affirmation and bent slightly over the steering, concentrating all his attention on evading the large tree roots that often protruded from the surface of the road in the woods.

Having reached the highway, we accelerated to high speed. It felt good to travel fast with the fresh air and the wind beating our cheeks. I carefully observed the sky, which was clear as a tear and blue like a calm sea, but I was not primarily interested in its beauty. I was searching for German airplanes. We had already gone about twenty kilometers and the wide yellow ribbon of the road lay in front of us, straight and empty of vehicles and men. But under the broad round crowns of the linden trees which lined both sides of the highway, there rested groups of harried people who, with their belongings, were escaping the oncoming Germans. From time to time the olive-green uniforms of soldiers were also noticeable in the shade of the trees. Those were the patrols and lookouts who were securing their units, and they looked at us, their eyes expressing a sleepy tiredness.

We were stopped by the military field police in a small town through which we had to pass, and our documents were checked quickly but thoroughly, together with our knowledge of the password for the day. The M.P.s warned us about low-flying German aircraft ahead of us.

"They are constantly patrolling the highway and machine-gunning it, when they see fit."

We thanked them and kept on going.

"The motor is drowning out the noise of the airplanes," I thought, and became all eyes. I didn't need to look long, for in front of us about three hundred yards away I saw the silvery silhouette of a Messer-schmitt 109 coming in low and directly toward us.

"Get under the tree!" I roared at Vlad. "The plane!"

The brakes of the motorcycle squealed as we suddenly swerved to the side from the middle of the road and came to an abrupt stop in the shade of the nearest tree, but in the same split second I heard the high pitched whistle of bullets hitting something with heavy thumps, and the crackle of broken tree branches, cut off by the bullets and falling on our helmeted heads. Dust rose from the road along the long line where the bullets were hitting its surface. I turned around to observe the passing airplane and saw him turning around.

"He is returning!" I shouted to my driver. "Get to the next tree! And slowly, so that you leave no dust behind us!"

Executing my order perfectly without raising any dust, the chauffeur moved three trees away from the spot where we had first stopped, but the long machine gun salvos resounded again over our heads and the German pilot, after the second run, was returning again.

"Get going! Slowly, otherwise we will get it!" I screamed again. This time Vlad put us only two trees farther.

Seven more times did our would-be executioner fly over us. Each time he chopped up the trees and road with his bullets, but each time he turned we "jumped" one, two or three trees away from our previous hiding place. Finally he turned west to return no more.

"Maybe his ammunition gave out," said the chauffeur. I was not too sure about it and only shrugged my shoulders.

We resumed our journey at high speed.

"How did you like the hide-and-seek?" I asked Vlad later. His answer came as a long litany of elaborate and even some rhymed curses which, if they could kill, would certainly have deprived of life not only this German pilot, but all his colleagues as well.

"We have been lucky, so far," I mused. "Perhaps all your wives are praying for your health?"

He sighed deeply and didn't say anything, but his face assumed such a happy expression that I was certain he must have been thinking about all his girl friends—or maybe only about the sweetest of them all.

We passed the guards of the divisional command post in Boratyn and delivered the message to the officer in charge. After having received from him the orders for the squadron we returned at once to our unit and we arrived there well before dusk and without incident.

Now began a period for my Falcon of uninterrupted travels at all times of the day and night, and it stood idle only when we had to wait at command posts for reports, orders, and assignments. Our journeys were often dangerous and we played a constant game of hide-and-seek with the German airplanes, becoming highly specialized at winning it, for losing it would mean death—and we didn't want to die. It was not a pleasant feeling to be constantly hunted and shot at by the better armed and practically untouchable enemy who sat comfortably in the pilot's seat and tried with ease to stop us or kill us. We must have been fortunate, because we didn't suffer even a single scratch from the uncounted German bullets fired at us.

We achieved great prowess in our riding and there were no impediments in the terrain which were too great. We learned how to ride through roadless woods, forests, ravines, hills and mountains. The rivers were no obstacles either. except that we had to find a ford shallow enough to pass over.

Sometimes, erroneously, we rode through territories already occupied by the Germans and once we were hailed as Germans, because that day we wore leather outfits and the villagers greeted us with ceremony and invited us to a festive and sumptuous meal, which we of course ate with gusto, while simultaneously planning their punishment.

During the meal some men talked to us in German, in such bad German that for the first time in my life I became proud of my knowledge of that language. The majority of the men from the village "reception committee" were drunk. Even Vlad's two word vocabulary of "jawohl" and "nein" fared well with them and facilitated the deception. Before the meal, to make sure that Vlad's lack of knowledge of the German language would not betray us, I admonished him severely to utter only those two words, but to eat and drink without an interruption, within reasonable bounds.

Finally the meal was finished and I had my course of action well planned. We stepped away from the table and drew our pistols. We brought the surprised herd of farmers to the village square. There we stripped them and taught them a lesson in patriotism: The flogging of one-half of them by the other, and then reciprocally, the flogged ones became the floggers. We barred the women and children from this show, about which we were not entirely happy either, but we felt that it had to be done. Some "patients" of that operation objected meekly, saying that we were repaying their hospitality with ingraditude, but we didn't take time to explain to the objectors the difference in application of hospitalities; we just told them that they could have been slower in showing their true colors. . .and we went our way. Suffice it to say that this village in the eastern half of Poland was not inhabited by Poles.

Once we arrested two deserters, whom we transported to the nearest M.P. headquarters. The next morning we were astonished indeed, to see the same two men walking unconcernedly along the road. They saluted us smartly in the military manner as soon as we stopped near them, but I clearly perceived their sanctimonious smiles and their certainty that we would not arrest them again. And they were right. We didn't arrest them. But we did use the same technique as with the villagers, and they had to flog each other until they grew tired. In addition, each had to repeat with every blow while flogging the other, "This is for your desertion from the Army!"

At another time we were fortunate in being able to bring to our lines a Polish pilot whose small sports aircraft caught fire before our eyes and landed in German-held territory. While rescuing him we almost "got it" from a German fighter plane, since we had to make our way back to our lines through open country. The Polish pilot was our colleague professionally. He performed liaison duties between two Polish army groups and we had to deliver him in a hurry to the garrison commander in Przemysl. Now, riding fast to Przemysl we joked with each other about the dramatic rescue.

On one occasion, when we were having a meal at the parish house in the small city of Grodek, some young college girls decorated our Falcon with flowers and did such a good job of it that it looked like a flower float at the Mardi Gras celebration in Nice or Cannes. We felt a little ridiculous riding with a flower shop, but on the other hand we couldn't simply discard the flowers that were offered us with such loving hearts. We found a quick solution to this problem. In the most elegant way, we handed out flowers to every girl whom we passed on the road, until there were no more flowers to give away.

Two differing moods were always working in us as well as in all the soldiers whom we met. Elation at still being alive, or the opposite—directed toward death. We saw death's "dance macabre," too often. But in spite of the fact that the air was permeated by the smell of burned corpses, that even the woods were filled with the odor of the decomposing flesh of humans or animals, or that we were followed by the smoke of blazing forests, towns and villages—we had not lost our hope and faith in life. We often buried dead soldiers whom we found in groves and woods, some of them having died recently, others a long time ago. We had to identify the dead; to be witnesses to the dying or the wounded whom we were unable to help; to deal with people who had become deranged due to their recent tragedies, who talked incoherently and shouted in the most horrible way imaginable. How many times did we become frightened ourselves?

More than once did it seem—especially under strong German fire—that this time we would "get it," that our end had come, that there was no way out for us to get out alive. But then it was our true friend the Falcon who carried us away from the midst of these bursting shells and hail of bullets. The Falcon was our salvation when searching out the units we were to contact, we found them destroyed—and were saluted instead by the blazing guns of German tanks.

The battles of Bircza and Przemysl, Mosciska and Sadova Vishnia, Stubno, Yaroslav and Dobromil were a few of the brighter points of the Falcon's performance that shone upon the darker background of unnamed, innumerable forest ambushes, chases and skirmishes, the attacks and retreats in which the Falcon had distinguished itself. Fast and nimble, the motorcycle became hardened under fire like a salamander, but his original colors changed into darker shades due to the extensive damage evident on its body, through which three bullets had already penetrated. Together with the numerous dents, the superficial damage was the best proof not only of its constant self-denying service, but also of endurance of the shower of shrapnel which found its mark from the top, front, back and both sides. The tin plates of the sidecar were also perforated by metal splinters, becoming looser with every passing day, and rattling with the vibrations of the rough rides. The motor never failed us, kicking over easily at the first gentle touch of the starting crank. Only once did it suffer a flat tire, but this was not even worthy of mention.

Fighting without interruption, we came to the huge forests of Yanov, where three divisions of Polish infantry, under fire for two weeks already, had to oppose seven German army groups, three motorized and four armoured. The woods stretching from Yaroslav to near Lvov were concealing in their depths both Polish and German forces, and our quick free movement was barely possible in the forests. Nevertheless, we still had to contact the many command posts and units whose movements needed constant coordination for action.

And—I remember it as if it had been only yesterday—one day we were speeding along a wide forest vista flanked on both sides by large trees, disregarding the uneven surface, for we were rushing to the divisional command post with urgent messages. In spite of our haste we carefully watched the numerous intersections and crossings, because, as we had discovered earlier, they could be full of unpleasant surprises. We had already arrived at the forestry office, where a control and information point was located, only about five kilometers distant from our destination. We were warned that the main highway we had to cross was in the hands of German armored units. We thanked our buddies for the warning and took off, slowing down a bit while approaching the critical spot. The road ran straight and descended rather sharply, so Vlad switched off the motor and we were approaching the highway as quietly as ghosts. Peace reigned all around us and we heard only at a great distance the deep grumbling of heavy artillery, muffled by the trees. Infrequently a machine gun crackled a short salvo not far from us.

We rode faster, for the drop in the road allowed the motorcycle to roll more quickly, still without power. I crouched in the sidecar, coiled and bent forward, pressing my right shoulder against the butt of the hand machine gun, my hand close to the trigger, ready to fire at a second's notice. Our eyes were strained until they started to hurt, ears alert, bodies tense. "What's in front of us?" was now the most urgent question. I concentrated totally, with all my senses.

The yellowish stripe of the highway was visible in

front of us at about forty yards and I forced myself deeper into my seat. My index finger touched the metallic guard around the trigger. Still twenty yards...and here we come...Suddenly, a loud roar seemed to destroy my ear drums, and another one and another...and the nearest salvos of machine guns appeared to shoot straight at our heads. At the first roar I instinctively opened fire, but I didn't see anybody, and I was shooting blindly to the sides of the vista, the motorcycle going at high speed. Vlad switched on the motor and with the gas on full we jumped over the highway. Without looking at it, for I was firing without a pause, or turning my head, I saw in a flash a long line of tanks and other vehicles standing on the hard surface of the road, and I was shooting furiously until there were no bullets left in the cartridge frame. I reloaded mechanically.

We reached the opposite side of the highway in a second and entered the forest through the same vista which continued in the same direction. I felt a sudden sting at my right knee, but no pain, and I continued to fire and stopped only when I emptied another magazine. It became quiet again and the noise of the motor was the only sound heard on the forest road. We looked at each other and Vlad smiled.

"Are you all right?" I asked him.

"Fine. All right. But that was some nest of vipers we just passed..."

We were riding fast when suddenly the motor coughed and choked, then started again and choked once more and came to a stop. Vlad jumped off nimbly.

"We shall see to it right away," he said and knelt at

the side of the motor looking at it carefully. I saw his face go chalk white.

"That's the end!" he said flatly. "It's all shot to pieces." He cursed and looked at me. "What's the matter with your leg? The blood..."

I bent over in order to see better. My right leg below the knee was covered with blood that soaked through the leg of my light-weight trousers. I felt uneasy and sat down on the grass in order to roll up the trouser leg.

"You got it in the leg," said Vlad with concern in his voice, and he came closer to me.

Only now did I feel a sharp pain in my knee. I gasped and clenched my teeth, while baring my leg. Of course, the blood ran from the knee and flowed freely down my leg. I turned to Vlad.

"Give me the bandages. They are in the sidecar under my seat in the first aid box. Be quick!"

And he was quick about it. I was able to stop the blood flow with firm pressure applied above the knee and it made me feel better. Carefully, I tried to locate the wound with my fingers, but instead I touched a hard object protruding from the knee into which it was stuck. "A grenade splinter," I thought with frightening dismay, for it could mean a serious chemical infection from the gunpowder—or, perhaps it is only a "clean" bullet? I tried to rationalize.

"What can I do?" asked Vlad.

"Plenty. Listen carefully: the divisional command cannot be farther than two or three kilometers from here. Straight on to the next intersection. You turn right there, cross over a brook and at about a kilometer from the brook on your left you'll find an old forester's hut—that's it. Repeat the directions."

He did it without an error and I continued: "Here are the reports and other documents"; here I emptied my large breast pocket of all the papers inside and handed them to him. "You have to deliver them personally to the aide-de-camp whom you know well. And ask him also to send someone for me. Hurry!" I tried to smile, but it didn't work. I was in pain.

Vlad looked at me in a funny way of concern and started at once, almost at a run. With difficulty I crawled away from the motorcycle and lay down in the shade of a large bush nearby. I became sleepy and realized that sleep was gaining the upper hand over my consciousness, for nothing else seemed to metter except to sleep...to sleep..."It is from the loss of blood". I attempted to fight the urge to sleep, knowing that I was not supposed to fall asleep while wounded and alone, but my attempts were faint and weak and my eyelids were becoming heavier, as if made of lead, with every passing minute, and it was difficult to keep my eyes open, the more so because the air was warm and fragrant with the sweetness of the foliage around me. I remembered my cigarettes and lit one, but it tasted repulsively bitter and sharp, and I extinguished it against the hard ground. Then I became thirsty and wanted a drink, but I recalled that our canteens were empty, and I looked with resignation through the leaves of the bush at the azure of the cloudless clean skies high above, and with the same resignation I listened to the salvos of the German machine guns. They were distinctly coming from the direction of the highway no more than a kilometer away. I tried to think. I wasn't aware of when I closed my eyes to protect them from the blinding rays of the sun shining in my face through the branches of the bush under which I was hiding. I relaxed completely, and a benevolent agreeable feeling totally overwhelmed me...

I half-heard some Polish words—buzzing like flies near my ears. I was laid on something cool and soft like a mattress, on which I bounced to the rhythm of the squeaking axle of a cart. Then a strong smell of ether almost woke me up, and I opened my eyes and saw some white walls and ceiling.

"Aha," I thought, "I am in a hospital..."

I knew that it was a dream and not reality when I saw my brand new Falcon. It started to talk to me in a loud voice which came from the small elaborate grating on the fancy horn: "Come," it said, "and look for yourself. I am the same one who got it on the forest road where you also got it in the knee. I am still the same, they only freshed me up and gave me some new clothes. Here, look into the sidecar where your cigarettes are still waiting...Your blood is still in the front of your seat, mixed with my sweat and my blood...Don't complain about your little bullet wound, for I was also wounded and didn't complain at all...And now, look, how well I function now...!"

I came close to him and gently kicked the starting crank. The motor switched itself on instantly and my chauffeur-friend appeared out of nowhere.—"Vlad," I was telling him, "this time we'll not let the Germans shoot up the Falcon...watch it!" I shouted. "The airplanes...get under the tree...slowly..."

I felt cold and shivered and my teeth chattered. A feminine voice was telling me something and I tried hard to understand the words, but I could not.

"Oh," it came to me, "this is the same young lady who with her girl friends decorated the Falcon in Grodek," and I wanted to thank her for her sweetness, but I couldn't get my voice out of my throat. This frightened me and I felt cold again. Then I saw the burning houses in Sadova Vishnia and the first dead soldiers near Medyka...and I cried, but I didn't feel cold anymore; on the contrary, I felt that my face, my hands and all of my body were covered with a hot, sticky, unpleasant sweat and I wanted to drink, but I knew that there was no water in the canteens...some German soldiers were coming at me and their helmets looked funny and I was aiming carefully and shooting at them. I knew that I must have scored direct hits, but they kept coming closer and closer and I wondered why I couldn't stop them, and kept shooting. Finally everything became blurred and vague and I couldn't see anything anymore. All was stillness and quiet.

Something aroused me and I opened my eyes to see above me a pretty and patient feminine face. It was encircled by the wide white wings of a monastic headdress.

"You will get back to your motorcycle," the nun was telling me as sweetly and gently as if I were a little child who had to be soothed, "but now, please, drink this," and she touched my lips with the edge of a large glass. It smelled like a good bouillon, and suddenly I felt very hungry. I drank it all greedily and was given another full glass. "And now," she continued, "you have to sleep," and she said it forcefully in a peremptory tone of voice. I just smiled at her—and fell asleep at once. This time there were no dreams or nightmares...

The Polish Cavalry—a symbol of chivalrous military traditions which at the battle for Vienna in 1683 and at Somosierra under Napoleon won for itself the distinction of being the world's finest.

MY FIRST HORSE

My first horse almost cost me my head.

In the first days of the September, 1939 campaign there was order and discipline within all Polish armed forces units. It was unthinkable for any soldier to discard any—absolutely any—part of his military equipment. The most valuable of all was an army rifle, for there simply were not enough rifles to arm the hundreds of thousands of young volunteers who were hanging around the military headquarters, city command posts, garrisons, army reserve offices, etc., etc. The German bombings resulted in the death of many of Poland's armed personnel, as well as the retreat of the Polish Army toward the east, and seriously increased the shortage of arms.

The second most valuable item of the military equipment was the horse—transportation for soldier and civilian alike.

All the roads in Poland became jammed with throngs of people escaping the oncoming Germans and communications between the West and East became a nightmare. Not only state highways but district and county roads, town, village, forest roads and even the paths were jammed with thousands upon thousands of refugees, their cars and carts drawn by horses, or sometimes by oxen, all moving east towards the large city-fortresses which had been bulwarks of Polish defense in the past, or trying to join their families, friends or acquaintances in the east. In any case, they tried to evade the front line fighting or German occupation. They were urged on by information about German atrocities, killings, and subhuman behavior.

The roads full of civilians were bombed by the "heroic" German airforce, and woe unto the people caught in the bombings. The horse became the dearest choice of everyone who could ride. It was the horse which was capable of carrying one out of the middle of the mass slaughter, in any direction one chose, into a "peaceful" place. Not road-bound, the horse could travel through forests and fields, swim rivers and climb hills, and all one needed for him was grain, grass, and water. Grain was available in every peasant's barn at a cheap price; grass and water were abundant everywhere.

I watched two long army columns crossing the same point in two directions, one moving to the northeast and the other to the southeast. Amid the reigning confusion I saw an ownerless horse carrying an army saddle and a sabre, first standing idle, then after a while walking slowly away and starting to graze. I had been standing there for a long time. I was lost in the countryside. I tried desperately to ask any officer who happened to be passing for information about the headquarters of my squadron. My attempts were of no avail. On the contrary, in some instances I had to show my documents because some overcautious officer suspected me of being a spy. I explained that I had lost touch with my unit because it had been destroyed by German tanks. He let me go while still eyeing me suspiciously. I stood there hoping that someone would come along who could give me the information I needed. The ownerless horse slowly moved away, grazing. I followed him, took the reins and brought him back closer to the crossroads. It turned dark, but the columns were still on the move. Not until around midnight did the traffic stop. I was left all alone with the horse. I came close to him; he sniffed me, snorted and looked at me. I waited. Should I take him, or not? If I left him alone he would wander around until he found people or other horses. . .

I mounted him and he followed the reins. Where to? I remembered generally where I was, and that about forty kilometers east-northeast lay the city of Sambor. I had to get out of the Carpathian forests. I had no compass to locate directions, but fortunately for me the stars were bright in the sky and I had no difficulty finding the way. To lead the horse along the easiest passable route, however, presented a considerable problem.

Very slowly we moved east and every time we passed through a clearing I looked at the stars. Up hill and down again and down we went, slowly but steadily and only the stars, trees and a gentle breeze were our companions. It was close to 3:00 A.M. when we arrived at a small hamlet. I knocked at the nearest door. No answer. With urgency, I knocked harder.

"Who's there?" asked a man's voice.

"A soldier! Show me the road to Sambor! I am lost!"

"Wait a minute."

An old peasant emerged from the hut.

"Well" he started, "You go straight along the path from my house that winds along the brook. About half a kilometer from here you come to a larger village road. There you take a left and continue for another kilometer till you reach a road crossing. The road to your right leads to Sambor through three more villages. You cannot miss it."

"How far from here to Sambor?"
"About thirty-five kilometers."
"Thank you very very much!"
"God lead you!"
"Remain with God! Thanks again!"

We had been traveling slowly indeed—and no wonder. Through the forest, cross country, we couldn't make any time. But now, I thought, perhaps we could go faster. In the darkness I was lucky to discern a somewhat lighter stripe which was the path, with the brook whispering on our right. The ground was even. I squeezed the horse with my legs and touched his sides gently with my feet. He understood and at once he set into a trot. In no time we came to a road lying in the darkness like a lighted stripe. It had a harder surface and the horse's hooves sounded sharper. He neighed. "Salute," I answered him according to custom. He lifted his head and kept going, still at a trot. In a few minutes we arrived at the crossing. I stopped, for I saw a road sign and I approached it

42

MY FIRST HORSE

I ate; he talked. Young John returned and reported
that Michael was taking care of the horse. And the host
talked war, politics, economics, and village life. I ate as
much as I could and only from time to time nodded
assent. Finally, I could eat no more. I took a package of
cigarettes out of my pocket and invited my host to a
smoke. He took a cigarette, looked at it, smelled the
tobacco and smiled appreciatively. I gave him two more
packages I had with me and he took them after refusing
them at first. I stood up and asked how much I owed him.

"You must be joking!" he countered. "I told you
that we have plenty to eat! We gladly share our food with
those who are defending us. If you want to repay me,
please, sit down and let's talk some more, because I am
quite sure your horse cannot be ready yet, so we have a
little more time to chat."

I obliged, but this time I was talking almost as
much as he was, and we concentrated on politics and war.
But gradually my tongue became weary and slower. The
warmth of the room, its quietness after everyone had left
us after the meal, my own tiredness and lack of sleep over-
came me. I woke up all by myself and at first I didn't
know where I was or how long I slept in that soft chair.
In a few moments I gathered my senses, got up from the
chair and went out. My host was sitting in front of the
house in the midst of some young men who were standing
around him, talking to them. He didn't see me as I
approached the group and I was able to hear him saying:
"... and as I said before, again and again, we must
form a well-armed village guard in order to be prepared for

every eventuality. But I didn't tell you what eventualities! So I'll tell you now. First, the Ukrainians are murdering single Polish soldiers and even some small units retreating in disorganization! Second, they are burning some small Polish hamlets in our county—and mind you, they are less numerous than we! Third, some Polish civilians have disappeared from predominantly Ukrainian villages! Fourth, we had thirty-seven Ukrainian families in our village. Look for yourselves. Since yesterday they have all disappeared. Where to? To their Ukrainian brothers! To Ukrainian villages! To kill us! To help the German 'fifth column'! And last, who is going to defend us, when the whole Polish army is engaged in fighting Germans, and we are cut off from any immediate aid from a larger army unit? I am taking command and I want obedience from you! Blind obedience! I am the sergeant-major of the reserve and your mayor! And I demand that any and all of my orders be carried out swiftly and efficiently! Any questions?"

I stood there in the back of the group as if I were rooted to the ground. I didn't know that in this part of Poland the situation had become so grave. But here was ample proof.

"He is right! He's right!" I heard from the men in the group. "How about arms? And ammunition?" They questioned him.

"I have enough arms and ammunition and I can get more! Two large army units that passed close by provided them and brought them straight to my house. They warned me about the Ukrainian killers, for they suffered casualties from an ambush not far from here! I will distribute the arms, but first I must organize a fighting force from among those of you who have served in the army. I want all able-bodied men to assemble here at noon sharp. So go now and fetch all of them and make sure they come!"

I glanced at my watch. It was 10:23 A.M.

The men nodded agreement and voiced approval of the mayor's plan as they began to disperse. My host stood up from his stool and saw me smiling at him. I raised my hand to my cap and saluted him. He returned the salute and came to me.

"Did you hear everything?" he asked.

"The most important part, I am sure."

"Don't you want to remain with us?"

"Sorry! I have to report to the nearest army unit. In Sambor! I have to find my squadron and my division!"

"Yes, I know you must attend to your duty. When do you plan to ride to Sambor?"

"Right away!"

"Well, I wanted to keep you here for a few more hours so that you could see us in action, or in preparation for action! I am sure you would like what you would see!"

"I don't have any doubt about it. You are doing a very fine job! For the glory of the Homeland!"

"For the glory of the Homeland!" he stood at attention while answering this patriotic formula which came from our hearts.

"Well! I'll have to say 'so-long.' Thanks again!"

''Do be careful while riding. There is only one forest between here and Sambor.''

''How many kilometers to Sambor?''

''Oh, about nine, not quite that many! There is your horse.'' He was pointing with his hand.

I turned around following his movement and I was astonished at the sight of a splendidly shining animal whom I scarcely recognized as the same horse who had brought me here. He had been cleaned in the most careful manner imaginable; his tail was braided and so was his mane. The saddle shone brightly and the stirrups looked as if they were made of nickel.

''How much should I give the man for taking care of the horse?''

''Do not offend him by offering him money. Give him a pack or two of your cigarettes!''

''That's not enough! I should pay him!''

''Don't offend him! He was a sergeant and a riding instructor.''

''Well! I'll be darned!''

The man brought the horse to me. I saluted him. He smiled at me and asked whether he could mount the horse. I said yes. He mounted without any visible effort—lightly, nimbly and gracefully. I envied him. He circled twice around us at a trot. My mouth must have been open wide, for I was watching a miracle of excellent horsemanship. The rider and the horse created an ideal unity. The horse was moving under him with elegance, pride, and quite aware of being watched! My host was looking at my expression, and he liked what he saw.

MY FIRST HORSE

The sergeant rode to us and dismounted.

"A fine horse you have." He turned to me. "But you didn't take care of him! How come?"

"I got him only last night, or rather this morning," and I explained to him how I had acquired the horse.

"Sorry! I didn't know! I hope you will be able to keep him—he is a fine animal. I have to compliment you also on another account!"

"Oh?"

"Before you sat down to your own breakfast, you worried about the horse! John told me!" He smiled broadly with approval.

"Well, you see, I like animals very much!" I felt myself blushing with an agreeable embarrassment.

"The more you know people, the more you like animals." The sergeant quoted the same old Polish proverb I used so often myself defending our four-legged friends.

"That's about how it is," interjected my host.

"I know I would offend you offering you money, so please accept this trifle as a proof of my gratitude." I held out three packs of cigarettes to the sergeant.

"Hm, Dameses! Very good cigarettes! Thank you very much!"

"It is I who thank you!"

I saluted and I looked at him. His face showed satisfaction.

"It is good that you don't have spurs. He works splendidly without them!" he exclaimed.

"And he doesn't get hurt by them, either!" I retorted.

"God lead you!"

"Remain with God!   And thanks to both of you!"

They both saluted me and I returned the gesture. We took off at a slow trot and the horse liked it. It was his best and easiest speed, and I was not supposed to tire him.

In about an hour we reached the small city of Sambor, which was now full of soldiers, command posts, cars, and traffic jams. I reported at once to the commanding officer, who informed me of the whereabouts of my squadron command post. It was located nearly twenty kilometers northwest of us. I thanked him and left.

At about 3:00 P.M. I arrived in Nizhauk and found my unit. Zbig saw me at once and came running.

"Where did you **steal him?**" he shouted, eyeing the horse.

"You know, I don't know myself," I answered and told him the whole story. We went looking for the soldier who was attached as ordnance-servant to the squadron commander, and I asked him to take perfect care of my horse from then on. He would not only not regret it, I emphasized, but he would have no reason whatsoever to complain of my lack of gratitude. With a joyous face the soldier took my horse, complimenting me on his appearance as he went.

I found a quiet place in a hut to relax, and I fell asleep straight away, confident that Zbig would wake me without fail when darkness set in and the squadron could move without risking German air attacks.

It seemed only minutes later that I was rudely

awakened by a soldier telling me that the squadron was moving out. My watch indicated 7:10 P.M. and it was getting dark. Within seconds I was ready, for I hadn't undressed. I ran to the squadron commander's quarters where my horse was standing, already saddled to march. In no time we were on the road moving north toward the city of Przemysl.

There was a stop soon at a crossroads to coordinate the crossing of several army columns. It was lit up by one single torch held high above his head by a mounted soldier. These crossings were a real problem, for each unit attempted to take priority. The problem was generally solved by the physical presence of a staff officer of the division or army group. If there were no such officer present, control was provided by the highest ranking officer, who effected the crossing of his own unit, naturally, and supervised it. But if during this operation a higher-ranking officer of another unit appeared, he took command and simply reversed the crossing order, giving his unit priority. We waited impatiently, cursing the delay first silently then louder and louder, until finally our turn came.

In a column three horses abreast I had the right flank, and our trio had just passed the center point when we were stopped by three riders, a lieutenant and two N.C.O.s.

"Where did you get that horse?" one of the N.C.O.s shouted at me.

"I found it ownerless last night!"

"You are lying! You stole it!"

"No! The horse was all alone for more than three hours and was running loose!"

"That's a lie!" shouted the lieutenant.

"You are a liar yourself!"I shouted back,seeing that the first lieutenant of our squadron was approaching fast.

"What's the trouble?"he shouted. "You are blocking the column! This is impossible! Move off the road! Off the road! On the side! Column march, march!"

Movement was restored again, while our first lieutenant and the three riders shouted at each other, each trying to make his point. The first lieutenant took my side, for he knew the story of my horse from Zbig, but at one point in the argument he opened the holster of his revolver when he saw in the unsteady light of the torch that one of the N.C.O.s threateningly opened his. He was the owner of "my" horse. Was he right in reclaiming "his" horse which he had permitted to wander away from him? That was an act of negligence for which he could be severely punished, especially during the war: "Neglect of army property!" And he already had another horse! I decided that I was right in "protecting" the army's property and I didn't make any bones about it.

"You do not deserve a horse!" I shouted, my rifle in my hands. "You don't know how to care for one! You allowed him to get lost! Did you spend last night with a slut? You aren't a soldier—how did you become an N.C.O.? Or are you nuts?"

They became silent, but my first lieutenant rode closer to me and dismounted.

"Give him back his damned horse. I will find you another!" he said with authority.

I bowed my head and felt like crying.

"Come!" he continued more softly, "our squadron is about to move. You will ride tonight with the headquarters train!"

The carbine still in my hands I dismounted. I looked at the horse and did not feel ashamed of my eyes full of tears. I turned quickly around in the direction of my squadron riding by. The last of the column was passing us. The headquarters train stopped at the lieutenant's signal. I mounted the high step and joined the engineer. Only then did I look back at my horse being led away by the N.C.O. I sighed deeply and sadly. Mine for all too short a time, I had lost a magnificent friend.

Breeding of Arabian thoroughbreds in Poland for about 300 years has produced highly valuable strains.

MY SECOND FOUR-LEGGED FRIEND

The morning was sunny and bright and there was no German bombing or strafing—only a blue cloudless sky. Our column moved slowly on a sandy road connecting two villages. I was riding in the squadron headquarters' car and looking aimlessly at the plain monotonous landscape around us.

Suddenly there was a sharp sound of neighing horses—and they came flying past us, more in the air than on the ground—only puffs of sand kicked up by their feet were proof that they were also touching the road. There were two of them, both as white as milk, free as birds, joyous as little children, fire in their eyes, wind in their manes, tails whipping the air. A moment later they disappeared behind the hill which we had just passed and the gaze of every soldier followed them in awe.

Within a few seconds half a dozen army riders followed them at a high gallop. Were they chasing them? It certainly looked so.

Again the stillness reigned all around us as we kept moving on. Having been on the march and cold the whole previous night, I fell asleep in the warm sun and was dozing peacefully on the comfortable seat, when horses' neighing woke me up and I turned toward the noise. Here they came, the same white wonders! This time they were not flying, but led by riders.

"Whose horses are they?" I asked one of the N.C.O. s who accompanied them. "What are you going to do with them?"

Before answering, the addressed man looked at me quizzically, to determine my interest in the horses. Apparently I didn't pass his examination, because he said slowly:

"You, sir —you surely will not be able to ride them. They have never had a rider on their backs and they are not even shod. They are from the State Military Stud Farm and we are going to do our darn best to break them in and to put them to work for the squadron."

"Why do you think I would not be capable of riding them?"

He gave me the superior smile of a horseman who knows what he is talking about: "After they are broken in, which is quite a job, only a professional rider or a first class horseman will be able to carry on. They would never perform for any amateur and if he tried, he would soon sorely regret his stupid daring! Even a good cavalryman would have his hands full with any of them. They need both a strong hand to handle them and sometimes an extreme softness, but above all they have to have someone who knows what and when!"

"Thank you. That was a very interesting lecture."

"Oh, don't mention it. The pleasure was mine!" He saluted me politely and departed, still smiling.

I was not a professional rider, and only an amateur, but my horsemanship was not too bad. His words and especially those white horses were now becoming a challenge. They were on my mind the whole long day. In the

MY SECOND FOUR-LEGGED FRIEND

evening I spoke to the second in command of the squadron about the white horses, expressing interest in acquiring one of them for liaison duties. The officer, less doubtful of my personal ability to handle horses, expressed no particular interest.

"Twenty-four hours will be sufficient for the trainer to work with them," he said slowly, but the rest will be up to you. The sooner you get the horse the better for you in the long run, because you will have to accustom him to your riding habits before somebody else does it. Well, report to me tomorrow at about 5:00 P.M."

Needless to say those twenty-four hours were the longest during my whole September 1939 campaign. I was thinking hard and asking hundreds of questions of soldiers who, according to my previous observations, were good riders and I deliberately avoided the N.C.O. In my opinion, he wanted to impress me and show off or to overwhelm me with his "I know it all" attitude extended to the point of discouragement.

Well before 5:00 P.M. I reported to the squadron command post. To my surprise I saw one of the white wonders standing in front of the house, impatiently stepping from foot to foot, neighing and trying to get his head loose from the grip of a sergeant who held his rein firmly. I was certain the sergeant was waiting to assess the horse's new rider, for he eyed me curiously before saluting me. In the next moment he assumed a carefree and unconcerned look as if he were expressing the thought: "No it cannot be him—he doesn't look like a stud tamer..." I smiled inwardly, but at the same time had serious misgivings. "Maybe the sergeants, both of them—the one who told me about the difficulties of riding this unshod stud and this one holding the horse—are right; perhaps I will not be able to handle him after all! And now the questioning expression on the face of the squadron commander's assistant! Imagine their laughter after I prove unable to manage the horse! How shameful for me! Now is the time to tell the officer that I have changed my mind! That I have a headache, a stomach-ache, any ache!

"Whoa! Slow down, Bobby boy!" I said to myself, "Slow down. Nothing is lost! I must do my best with the horse, and if I see that I cannot handle him I can always ask a good rider to assist me and to keep close to me in the case of need...!"

I saluted briskly and reported my arrival. The officer smiled at me.

"Well,—he is all yours! Watch out for him and for yourself. I hear he is quite a temperamental Arabian. His family tree papers are longer than those of some of the German aristocratic families! Take good care of him!"

"Yes, sir!" I saluted and left the room. I walked somewhat stiffly and officially toward the sergeant with the horse.

"By order of the squadron commander the horse is assigned to me!" I said curtly and took the reins from his hand. The gaping face of the soldier was ridiculous with astonishment. I could not help but smile while saluting him. He remained standing there with his hand in the air as if he were still holding the reins. The horse followed me with ease. I felt somewhat relieved. I was leading him around the house into the back yard, for I didn't want to have any witnesses to any eventual "accident" that might happen when I mounted him. I stopped and he did the same. I took out of my pocket two pieces of hard lump sugar and offered them. He ate them with gusto while I checked the saddle and the stirrups. I came to the horse close from the left, put my left foot in the stirrup and mounted. He moved some and neighed lightly. I caressed his neck, eased the reins and he lifted up his head. I gave him a gentle shove with my feet and moved forward. I rode the horse around onto the village street. The soldiers were getting ready to start the march, but every one of them looked up at the sight of the milky white steed. I felt very proud of him and, of course, of myself too!

Two hours later I received reports from the squadron command for quick dispatch to the divisional headquarters. I set on my way immediately. Having studied the map carefully I knew which roads to take and despite the oncoming darkness I was sure of finding my destination without difficulty. It took about five hours to reach the division command post and after having delivered the documents I was told to rest until the next morning when new orders for the squadron would be ready for dispatch. I was too tired to look for civilized quarters and, anyhow, I was dead sure that all the houses and huts in the village were occupied, because it was a small locality. It was late and I knew that to find shelter I would have to wake half of the village. I resigned myself to sleep under the stars. For the first time during the whole campaign I was warm at night and I slept well. I was warm because my horse had lain down, an act which

I could not understand then. It was explained to me later that many fine stud horses preferred to lie down to sleep rather than to sleep standing up, and I lay down next to him so that his belly was warming me better than a featherbed. When I woke up I was lying face up, but I couldn't see the sky—only the close belly of my waiting horse. He must have gotten up so gently that I had not awakened. Now, I was lying straight, my head almost between his front legs and my feet between his hind legs. Very gently I crawled out from under him, and some soldiers smiled while telling me that it was quite a picture to see us sleeping together, close to each other, and then me alone beneath him. I smiled back at them and praised his gentleness. I was proud of him.

After breakfast I took the orders from the divisional aide-de-camp and set out on my way back to the squadron. The previous night I had ridden very slowly—first, because it was dark; second, because I didn't know the horse. I had noticed during that first encounter that his steps were short, which was no surprise at all, for he was not a big Percheron or Polish-bred horse, but a fine delicate Arab, small-boned, graceful, sensitive, gentle and mischievous as a little child.

This was the first time that I had to make an extended ride in the broad daylight, a prey to the German pilots who tried to kill everything that moved on the roads. A lonely rider was automatically considered by them to be a courier or liaison carrying orders, reports or other military documents. An additional hazard for me was the color of my horse, which could not be blended into the physical surroundings. Of all the colors, white

MY SECOND FOUR-LEGGED FRIEND

was the worst. I felt this at once when a strafing German aircraft began to work over the village through which I was riding. With his machine guns blazing, the pilot came at low speed. His ammunition seemed to be as inexhaustable as his zest for shooting at the village. What he was after I didn't know. I took cover under a low-branched and wide-spread large linden tree where some soldiers had already found protection.

"What the hell do you think you are doing?" shouted one of them angrily at me. "May the devil take your horse! Get that damned animal out of here! Quick! We will all get killed! He can be seen for miles!"

I didn't answer. I just took my submachine gun off my shoulders and held it under my right arm with the barrel facing my adversaries. My pointing finger was close to the trigger and I let my horse loose on long reins.

"Listen, you son-of-a-bitch!" I shouted, accentuating strongly each syllable and forgetting a long-ago promise made to myself that I would never curse anyone with the name of an animal contained in the curse because, in that case, I was injuring the animal and complimenting the man about to be cursed. "It doesn't make any shitty difference to me whether your cowardly carrion is gotten by the Germans or by me! Are you that blind that you don't see that he"—here I pointed at the plane—"is not after us, but after something else in the village? And don't you try anything stupid," I added a quick warning, for I noticed a sudden movement within the group, "because I have enough ammunition in this little submachine gun to send you all to heaven!" Nobody moved any more, and I was sure that none of them realized before I said it that my smallish looking weapon was a deadly submachine gun. "Sit down, darn you, and relax!" My eyes addressed only my single outspoken adversary, but my words were directed to anyone who might object. A young soldier with a kind, gentle face left the group and approached me slowly. He was not armed, and I sighed inwardly with relief.

"A fine horse you have there! Oh, a stud!" he said, coming closer and admiring him openly.

"Yes. Thank you. Hold him for a moment." I passed him the reins and stepped sidewise out of the protecting shade of the tree to gain a better look at the German airplane that kept diving and shooting at something in the middle of the village.

"All of you stay here," were my orders to the soldiers, "and keep the horse close to the tree trunk, if you are afraid. It is impossible to see him or you from the air. I am going to see what seems to interest that pilot so much. Maybe I can help there! The horse better be all right when I return or else..." Here I touched my gun menacingly. "And I make you, young man, responsible for reporting to me any cowardly behavior of anyone here," I added slowly and solemnly. The soldier nodded his head in affirmation. The others in the group remained silent, and I walked out at a fast pace, glad to have resolved an unpleasant situation. "May the cholera take them," I muttered the Polish curse under my breath while wondering at the ease with which all those curses were coming to me, for I seemed to learn to use such obscenities rather quickly. But I felt disgusted and my stomach contracted unpleasantly.

MY SECOND FOUR-LEGGED FRIEND

Now I had to leave such thoughts behind, because I had to reach the village. I ran fast toward the nearest house, knowing that the risk I was exposing myself to was practically non-existent. I knew how to evade the danger from enemy planes. I discovered and practiced an evasion technique which was very simple and consisted of always having something between the airplane and myself, for instance, a house, a wall, a thick tree trunk, anything, even a large rock, a pile of wood or a bomb hole. And I had to keep the airplane constantly under observation. Only a very close bomb could get me, but I was sure, as sure as I could be—as I had practiced it in the past with success on all occasions, for otherwise I would not have been alive—that I could always outrun the falling bombs and quickly find an obstacle to put between me and them. Of course, it had worked well in the past and I was confident that it would be so in the future.

At the moment there seemed to be no great danger because the pilot's machinegunning was directed to points two hundred or more yards distant. I ducked momentarily when some bullets, probably stray, hit the ground right in front of my nose, but I consoled myself that they must have been aimed at something else and I kept running faster along the line of village houses. Now I could not see the plane and I had to use my ears instead of my eyes, thus I attempted not to make much noise as I ran. There was a sudden roar..., a hail of bullets around me and I threw myself in the ditch close by. Then stillness...I got up and started to run again, only to be stopped in my path by the debris of a freshly destroyed barn. As I tried to circle around it I heard voices close by:

"Halt! Halt!" I froze in my tracks and looked for the people who were shouting, but in vain. I couldn't see anybody.

Again the plane's noise came nearer and I jumped behind a large pile of timber. The bullets hit close and it became quiet again. I got to my feet, turned around the corner of the heap of timber and within five yards I saw an anti-aircraft machine gun position manned by three soldiers working feverishly at the gun. I walked up.

"What's up?" I asked. None of them turned. After a while one of them answered:

"It's jammed. We're trying to clear it!"

"What a shame! We could get him if the gun were operational!"

"Maybe we still can!"

"Anything I can do to help?"

"Yeah! Start praying—and get lost!"

I stood there smiling to myself at their bravery and complete lack of concern about the strafing aircraft. It came again spitting fire from its guns. We all hit the dirt. As the plane passed they went right to work on the gun.

"Hurray!" exclaimed one of them suddenly. "We've done it! We've got it! Let's get the bastard!"

The barrel of their machine gun moved smartly toward the sun—the source of the attacks. The noise of the plane's motor came closer and I felt the tension of the three soldiers.

"Now!" shouted one of them.

The explosions from the anti-aircraft machine gun became so deafening I had to open my mouth. I looked up at the passing enemy craft. With a convulsive jerk it pulled up and away—out of sight behind the hill. We waited for its return, but its motor became fainter. It slowly faded away.

Only then did the soldiers take notice of me. I saluted on seeing a captain's epaulets on the shoulders of one of them.

"What are you doing here? And who are you?" he barked.

I reported, identifying myself and asked the reason for such ferocious strafing of the village. The captain gave me a stare and led me about fifteen yards from the gun position onto the wide village street. There stood three fire engine trucks, shot to pieces by the German pilot. Despite the damage, they retained their shiny, eye-hurting, highly polished, brassy look.

"The pilot must have taken them for something worth destroying and hit them with everything he had, including incendiary bullets," explained the captain, "but they refused to burn. They were all out of gas—not even a drop—but full of water. Ha. Ha. Ha. He took quite a chance flying as low as he did. He was just lucky our machine gun jammed...but due to his ferocious attacks on the fire engine, many lives were saved. Not one villager was even wounded because they all ran for the woods after his first strafing. Poor old fire engines..." he finished his explanations with a chuckle.

I thanked him and rushed back to the linden tree. No one was there anymore, except the young soldier grazing my horse.

"Sir!" he said to me. "You could not imagine the wrath you have caused! If their wishes came true you would be dead by now—and not only once. They all took off like scared rabbits. They were afraid of you. Only one of them had a rifle. They were deserters going home—all Ukrainians. You were lucky! They wanted to kill you and they threatened me, too!"

"I see. Where is your unit?" I asked.

"We got it from the Germans in Grodek and this is the first village I have come to since the battle. German tanks broke through our lines and we were encircled. I will report for duty to any unit I meet!"

I told him about the captain. He went with me to the machine gun position. After introducing him to the officer I left in a hurry. Carefully avoiding the hard surfaced roads—my horse was not shod—I worked my way back to the squadron.

As soon as I slept and ate I reported for orders. My schedule became very hectic. I carried reports to the division and brought divisional orders back to the squadron. I had to memorize the content of each and every message for the eventuality of being apprehended by the enemy. In this case I was to eat the message and to pretend that I was a straggling soldier. Division messages assigned to the squadron various contacts with the enemy and reconnaissance of the enemy positions and movements, whereas those from the squadron reported to the Division all resulting information.

I came to like my horse and to admire him, but I noticed that he was too frail and delicate for such rugged service. I welcomed the initiative of my commander who proposed a change of horses.

MY SECOND FOUR-LEGGED FRIEND

"But sir, what will happen to the milky white?" I asked.

"He will be given to a farmer who needs his stud services," the captain answered calmly. "It is no problem at all. Any farmer will take him gladly and even be willing to pay handsomely for him."

I took the milky white to the commander's train with a rather heavy heart, but feeling certain that the days of excessively heavy duty for my horse were over and that he was coming to a well deserved advancement. The military marches, lack of sleep, improper food and care simply unjust to him.

I was offered a choice of a dozen splendid, heavy-boned, Polish-bred horses whose owners had perished in battle. In that instance at least, the animals didn't pay the price for human mistakes. The horses were kept in the rear, generally well protected for they were the last hope for an escaping soldier.

During the campaign I lost count of the days of the week. It was simply not necessary to worry about the day of the week. What difference did it make whether one died on Sunday or Monday? I ceased to feel hungry and lost my appetite—perhaps because I began smoking. It started during our marches through bombed and burned cities, towns, villages and forests—with the most horrible stench of human and animal flesh burning and rotting. Every time I smelled it, questions came to mind. Whose flesh is it? Human or animal?

During the whole campaign I didn't take a bath. This is hardly complimentary to my personal hygiene, but there was neither time nor opportunity. I changed my

underwear frequently and in addition I used perfumes
and cologne water as disinfectants with excellent results.
In all the filth and dust and while sleeping in places infest-
ed with bedbugs, flies, and lice, my skin did not show the
slightest rash or insect bites. And, wonder of wonders—
I did not get tired! Sleepy—yes, but tired—no! I must
have had the strength, endurance and stomach of a horse!
Well, that's youth!

THE THIRD WAR HORSE

This time I had a say in the choice about to be made. But it was a difficult choice indeed, for all the horses had been carefully selected before the war for service in cavalry units. Among their many colors, chestnut prevailed, but my ideal was a gray horse for reasons of personal and animal safety. The gray, perhaps, blended best with the environment. I began to regret the fact that horses don't come in a green strain, for it would have been the safest color of all—mixing into the greenery of the surroundings! I certainly would have selected a "dirty green" shade. But I also knew that I could cover him in case of emergency, as had seen others do recently, with a green army blanket or overcoat. I didn't spend a long time making up my mind. A gray gelding, whom I came to like at first sight was my choice. I led him away from the stables and he followed me with brisk steps. Every horse, like every human being, has his personality, and I noticed at once his fine temperament from his keenly alert eyes, from the way he was stepping, holding and moving his head and swishing his tail. I was satisfied. I mounted him at once and let him go into a trot. He was excellent! The difference between the former stud and the grey proved remarkable, for he carried me like a large ship carries one on the waves. His long strides felt good and I relaxed happily, remembering the stud's short steps that shook me up constantly. Thus I began the third week of war—bearing signs of defeat.

One day Zbig and I read the leaflets dropped by German planes announcing in horribly bad Polish that the Soviet army crossed the borders of Poland from the east. We didn't believe a word of it, for we knew very well that Poland had a non-aggression treaty with Russia. Only after many days did this solemn and eventful news become a certainty. Even then we still were not aware of the attitude of the Red Army toward us. It was soon clarified.

More and more soldiers without arms were visible on the roads, but they were still asking for their units; we simply sent them in an easterly direction to the nearest cities because we knew that the Army had to reorganize somewhere in the east. Firm purpose still existed in these soldiers' questions, no matter how tired and sleepy they were. Many were covered with wounds and bloody bandages. Remembering that the city fortress of Lvov had never surrendered to enemies in past wars, we also directed the soldiers to that city.

German airplanes became a daily menace. It was really a game of "hide" without "seek" that we constantly played with them. To win it—meant staying alive. To lose it—well, we got accustomed to death. She seemed to be present everywhere and our senses became even duller to the sight of human suffering when we realized that we could be of no help to the wounded and dying no matter what we did. The railroad lines and stations were bombed and shot to pieces, together with the railroad bridges and the ordinary river bridges. Many hamlets, villages and towns ceased to exist. They were totally burned out. Any city through which our way led was heavily damaged or partly destroyed either from the air or by ground artillery fire. The disorder of the military columns caught by German planes was indescribable, especially when they mingled with throngs of civilians who were escaping east. The scenes of Dante's Inferno seemed innocent compared to what we saw of the bombed and machine-gunned defenseless refugee population. Men, women, children, babies, soldiers, cars, baby carriages, horse and oxen carts, bicycles, hospital wagons, evacuated civil servants of innumerable municipalities, police and fire department personnel, administrative officials in uniforms or without them, some in winter coats, others in summer dress— all this screaming mass of people and animals rushed away in heedless panic from the road being bombed and strafed from the air. The chaos assumed the proportion of a catastrophe with everybody for himself and only mothers clutching their children and babies...

We were more fortunate, because we didn't see many of those horrible, hair-raising tragedies. We were closer to the enemy—where it was soldiers who were dead and wounded. They knew about dying and suffering and their duty involved death.

We annihilated some German units and took numerous prisoners. On many occasions I was called to divisional headquarters to serve as an interpreter. Some Germans were wounded and afraid of dying, others cried from pain, but the uninjured ones looked upon us with contempt or outright hatred. Once I saw two Polish soldiers shouting at the prisoners, but officers intervened at once. Our general attitude toward them was one of a hostile correctness. On quite a few occasions I observed Polish guards showing their prisoners leniency and I thought it good, for one never knew whether soon the situation would be reversed. All the prisoners were kept in the immediate vicinity of the headquarters.

We also gained some valuable German booty: armored cars, trucks, cars, motorcycles, arms and ammunition, food, tobacco, cigarettes and thousands of items which appeared to be great luxuries for they were packed in a rich and elaborate manner. The motorcycles were BMWs with foot clutches, so I showed others how to operate them. This time they were serving us against their previous owners, but unfortunately not for long. Our gasoline supply kept dwindling with no place to replenish the empty tanks and storage barrels. Eventually we had to abandon more and more mechanized vehicles and burn them.

After the bloody battle in the forests of Yanov we came to the small city of Bzhuch. Sleepy and hungry, we brought in our horses and threw ourselves on the straw and hay in the nearest barn we found. The early morning held a surprise for us. A young and pretty female teacher who noticed us sleeping there prepared us a nice breakfast. Disregarding the nearby battle in progress at the city outskirts, with machine gun and heavy artillery fire, we sat down and ate heartily. She asked us many questions about the war and political situation, but we had no consolation for her. We told her about the Soviet army marching into Poland and that it came to our assistance, according to some information, but that opposite opinions were gaining preference among the soldiers and civilians alike. Other news circulating among the population interpreted the Red Army's actions as cooperation with England and France. Our information was not quite believable, but we were repeating it exactly as it came to us. We commented that it was Red Army propaganda aiming to diminish the Polish resistance and to convince the Poles that it was cooperating with the Western powers. We also passed on to the teacher the general concensus among the Polish armed forces—that we had to face the fifth partition of Poland, that we were lost as a state and a nation, and that France and England would not make a move to help us. She started to cry and we tried to do our best to console her, in spite of the fact that we didn't know ourselves anymore what was the true situation. We stated that there was nothing we could do except to fight, no matter how—openly, or as conspirators and partisans— for after all, Poland had been enslaved in the past for over one hundred years by Prussia, Austria and Russia, but by fighting, it had gained freedom again.

While she cried quietly the din of the battle came alarmingly close. I looked through the window and froze for a split second—three German tanks were rolling sideways and shooting wildly. They were followed by infantry—all about fifty yards from the house we were in.

"Look, Zbig!" I exclaimed and he joined me at the window.

"To the horses!" he shouted and ran out.

"Wait a moment! I have to finish my breakfast!"

He must have been beyond the reach of my voice

already, for he didn't answer. I quickly ate some home-made thin rolls and drank the coffee and milk while simultaneously looking through the window with my eyes glued on the Germans. Their tanks and soldiers were bypassing the house by no more than thirty yards, shooting furiously at something in front of them and to the far side. I quickly swallowed the food and drink on the table.

"Thank you very much for your hospitality, Mademoiselle!"

"Don't go!", she started to cry again. "You will be killed! You have only a gun! Let me go out first and look . . " she begged through her tears.

"No, Mademoiselle! There is nothing there for you to look at! Don't worry! Nothing is going to happen to me! Good-bye! And thanks again!"

She stood at the window and cried silently. I quickly left the house through the back door opening into the courtyard, stopped abruptly at the exit and looked around. There were no Germans in view, but a heavy fire fight was raging all around. I ran to the barn looking for Zbig. His horse was gone, mine was standing at the spot where I left him, eating hay as peacefully as ever. I smiled to myself: "He has better control than I do!" I opened the heavy barn door and saw somebody moving out of the corner of my eye. Without thinking I aimed the submachine gun at the person only to lower it instantly: it was the pretty teacher running from the house to the barn.

"Anything I can do?" she gasped.

"You must be stark crazy! But hold the door ajar and close it the moment I leave! Where is the nearest forest? How far?" I asked her while mounting the horse.

"About three hundred yards! Straight this way!" she pointed with her hand. "It starts where my garden ends! You cannot miss it!"

I felt lucky once again and I knew I would make it. I put my horse into a gallop and as he was flying past the first trees of the garden I turned my head to her and saluted with my hand. She still stood at the door and waved at me. Now I had to concentrate on my horse, who was going fast, close to the trees on the somewhat uneven ground of the garden. Without the slightest hesitation he easily cleared two deep water ditches and was galloping at full speed toward a nearby, dense, dark-green woods. I rode with my head bent down in order to avoid low branches and kept my head still lower when we reached the forest.

I stopped the horse at once and looked back. The air was still full of flying bullets which seemed to come from all directions with their whining whistles. The heavier the weapons the deeper was the tone of the flying steel. The heaviest fire came from the western portion of the city. Dense smoke from burning houses lay thickly over it and naked flames shot straight up into the air. I dismounted and approached the edge of the forest trying to "read" the situation. There was not a person to be seen. The din of artillery shots, ear-shattering cracks of tank cannons and incessant heavy machine gun burping appeared to be threateningly near. Bullets were cutting leaves and small branches as well as some large ones from the trees and all the pieces of wood and greenery were falling on my head.

I was alone and had to look for somebody—for any military unit—because I knew that I could not quickly reach my squadron's command post forty kilometers distant. I decided on a southeasterly direction; that is, toward the city of Lvov, hoping to find organized resisance on my way. I mounted the horse and was making headway very slowly, for the forest was dense. I had to duck the low branches of trees and to master numerous small but steep ravines. When it became impossible to ride further, I had to dismount and lead my horse through heavy underbrush. After a while I found a path which led in the right direction and with relief, I rode again. Around noon I was still riding in the woods that seemed to have no end. Suddenly I smelled smoke and became very cautious. I came closer to the clearing and saw in front of me a burning brick factory. I tied my horse's reins to a tree, remembering the location, and carefully approached the bushes at the edge of the clearing. There was no one in sight and I began to circle the factory. At a few places I discovered some fresh soldiers' fox holes and breastworks. I moved slower attempting to go around the burning buildings. I thought there must be somebody nearby. The conflagration itself seemed to be fresh and someone must have started it not more than an hour ago, but I still saw no one. After about two hours I found myself in the same place from which I started, having found no one. I sighed, for I knew that I had to continue alone. I went to the tree where I had left my horse, but...there was no horse. I became alert and uneasy—a little scared, for I thought that somebody must have found and taken the horse. I approached the tree still closer and found the reins that slid down its trunk and were lying on the ground. Only then I realized that my horse had become afraid, liberated himself and run away, and I knew that he would not stop until he found other horses or people. I sighed again, picked up the reins from the ground and started walking. Fir trees emanated the sweet fragrance of their needles and flowers in small clearings perfumed the warm air with their aroma of live incense. The forest became peaceful, still and quiet. Only then did I realize how sleepy I was. I sat down in the grass and then lay down, knowing full well that I would fall asleep. I slept less than an hour, for the warmth of my body woke me up, and I noticed that I was sweating; no wonder, because the sun was still high and hot and the air seemed not to move. I removed my jacket, sweater and shirt and only then I felt comfortable and chuckled to myself at the thought of having a sun bath during the campaign. I remained in that meadow for another hour and wanted to stay longer, but for a while now I had been hearing the deep bass of heavy artillery. I resumed moving in the same southeasterly direction, remembering from the map that the Bzhuch forests end in the vicinity of Lvov. Because the air was hot and I was sad after the loss of my horse, I walked slowly and kept thinking about him and blaming myself for his loss, but there was nothing I could do. So I continued to walk with a heavy heart, all alone, half lost in the huge friendly forest, totally lost in my thoughts...

A display of Polish armored units and Air Force in 1939.

MY FOURTH WAR HORSE

Deep in the forest, the din of war was not audible. As I advanced, the woods were broken by clearings and meadows of ever increasing size. As I reached the edge of one of the open spaces, I heard voices and immediately hid in the underbrush, instinctively preparing to fire. A loud conversation was in progress. The language was Polish! I emerged from my hiding place and approached the group of soldiers. About forty of them were marching casually, as if they were on the way to a picnic. In response to my inquiries, a major and a lieutenant informed me that the group was attempting to reach Lvov. They asked me whether I knew the countryside well enough to lead the way. I answered affirmatively, for I remembered the map very well indeed. They told me that the soldiers came from various units and simply rallied around them for leadership.

I noticed that a soldier who kept to the back of the column was leading a horse, the only horse in the whole group. I moved closer to him.

"What do you want me to give you for that horse?" I asked.

"Oh, nothing, nothing at all! Take him if you like him. He is only an encumbrance and a burden to me, but nobody wanted him and somebody has to take care of him. Here. He is all yours!" he added quickly as if he thought that I might change my mind.

"Here are some cigarettes and tobacco in exchange —but I don't have any cigarette paper." I extended my offering and he took the cigarettes and tobacco with gratitude, objecting under his breath that it was not really necessary. Then he thanked me, again and again.

I was grateful to the soldier and glad that he was not a member of the cavalry. Otherwise he would surely have kept the horse. I was very pleased with my acquisition and looked him over carefully. He was a tall, long animal, almost black with an unusual tinge of navy blue so light that it was perceptible only when the sun's rays fell on him. His forehead bore a little white mark, resembling a white stamp or identifying mark of some sort. The contrast of this white stamp imparted beauty to his appearance. His eyes were alert and intelligent and he moved his ears smartly. He carried his long thick black tail proudly and arched gracefully like a Spanish woman with her ornamental fan. He walked with dignity, aware of his own worth, and his long steps were deliberate, seemingly the result of gentle consideration and seriousness.

Stopping to adjust the saddle and stirrups, I fell far behind the marching soldiers. I urged the horse into a fast trot. What a pleasure was that ride! With a gait similar to that of my previous mount, the new horse didn't bounce me at all but produced the impression of floating quietly through the countryside. In no time I overtook the battle column, passed it and was scanning the woods. Nothing stirred—everything was silent and so tranquil that I smiled to myself, remembering the morning hours in Bzhuch.

The forest road was pitted with holes and protruding roots from nearby trees, all covered with a thick layer of dust which readily recorded the footprints of tired soldiers. To our right and below us extended a valley whose opposite bank formed a steep ridge some hundred feet high. We were not able to see over the ridge but everything was very still. To our left was dense forest, always a friendly refuge from German airplanes, although we had not heard a single one during the whole day.

Suddenly from the high ridge on our right, we were assaulted by sharp fire from several machine guns. We instantly scattered into the woods and took cover from our attackers. There was not one machine gun among us except for my small submachine gun—obviously a great disparity in arms. The volleys from the ridge ceased as suddenly as they had begun and there were no further sounds from the enemy. I started to fire at brief intervals but there was no response from the Germans who preferred to ignore the challenge of my peashooter. They apparently chose not to waste ammunition by firing into the woods. I decided to follow their example since my salvos, loosed for their psychological effect, seemed pointless. I forgot that they would also signal some of our own men but only two of them showed up: the Major and the Lieutenant. We waited together for some time, talking in half-whispers, but no one else joined us. Evidently the other soldiers had adopted the most disorderly but the oldest principle, *every man for himself*. We saw no more of them. From the depths of the forest we caught the faint sound of twigs breaking under their feet. The noises grew more distant and soon ceased.

It was late afternoon, and we traveled due east, suspecting that on our right, atop the continuing steep ridge, there must be more German positions. I knew that we would have to climb the ridge eventually, but we decided it would be wiser to do it at night. In the meantime, we resolved to cover as much distance as possible.

With the early light we changed direction and headed due south. I began to entertain the possibility that we might not reach the city as easily as I had encouraged the others to believe earlier. I had begun to question my ability as a guide. The last time I looked at the operational map at division headquarters, I distinctly remembered the distance to Lvov, but it occurred to me now that by all calculations we should be very near the city already.

We suddenly heard the distinct sound of artillery from the southeast, south and southwest. I realized that my original impression had been correct. The Germans would be firing with this intensity only at the fortress of Lvov. We knew that there were no large army units or other targets in our immediate vicinity.

We waited for darkness to close in and climbed to the top of the ridge where we encountered several wires stretched along the ground. The wires resembled telephone lines, and we reasoned that they must be German, since the Poles never leave such wires on the ground but string them high on electrical poles and trees. There was also their direction. They lay due east to due west, an arrangement which would not have served the Polish units, since there were no substantial concentrations of Polish troops north of Lvov. They would not have needed east-west communications. We determined to cut the wires.

This was accomplished with some difficulty, since we had only pocket knives in our possession and the cables were relatively thick and strong.

"Look!" I exclaimed, pointing south.

"Lvov!" shouted the officers.

Indeed, we could discern distant fires which must have been caused by either German airplanes or artillery, probably during the daytime. The blazes were apparently buring uncontrolled. The people were probably in the shelters and cellars, and there were apparently not enough firefighters to extinguish the blazes.

We traveled directly toward them. I was not tired at all because I was riding, but the officers walked slowly. The crack of exploding artillery shells was becoming louder, but the fires were diminishing and after a while they died out. Only the din of artillery and the flashes of explosions continued. The terrain descended and became easier to cross. The night was dark and no stars appeared in the sky, so that we came upon houses of a village only by practically running into them.

"There must be Germans here," said the major, and we didn't contradict him. As if to affirm his statement, we heard the heavy thud of marching steps as they resounded against the hard surface of a nearby village road. By the volume of the sound, we could tell that the marchers were approaching steadily. We held our breaths and I squeezed harder on the halter of my horse to prevent him from neighing. It was easy for us to eavesdrop on the German conversation of the passing soldiers. The size of the column was impressive. It took some minutes for it to pass by.

"You ought to get rid of the horse," cautioned the major, "he could be dangerous, because now we are about to cross German controlled territory!"

After a short discussion, I gave in. I led the animal quietly to a small barn with its doors ajar. When I entered the building I smelled cows and heard their slow, deep and loudly peaceful breathing. When my eyes became accustomed to the darkness, I identified an empty corner where I tied the horse's reins to a sturdy cowstand. I unsaddled him and concealed the saddle beneath a heap of straw, then I slipped out of the barn as silently as possible. Surrounded by stillness, I carefully retraced my steps to the two officers who were waiting for me. It was hard to leave my friend alone—a friend that I had just acquired and whom I was now forced to abandon. The officers consoled me as best they could.

"When we reach the city," said the major, "I will make sure that you can have any horse that you want. Don't worry!"

I remained silent. I wanted no horse but my own. I had already named him Dan which means "given" in Polish. He was the only horse who meant anything to me. I concentrated upon the location of the small barn in order to remember it and resolved in my own mind to return for the horse later—that is, if I should still be among the living. I sighed and we continued our journey.

We walked without talking and crossed the road as well as a small rivulet in our progress south. Beyond the village we reached open fields and continued our tedious march up a gently rolling hill. The night grew darker and there were still no stars to direct us. A light rain began to fall, soon soaking us and slowing our progress since the footing became slippery and unsure. Nevertheless, the rain was a blessing.

All Poland had been praying constantly for the autumn rains which this year refused to fall. German heavy arms would be hopelessly bogged down when the meadows, fields and forests became marshy. Their mobility would be reduced to zero in the soft deep mud.

The night grew cold and we started to shiver. A large conflagration attracted our attention and we directed our steps straight toward it. The building in flames was a large brick factory, and I reflected that this was the second brick company that we had seen burning during the last twelve hours. We came close, removed our coats, jackets and caps and began to dry them in the intense heat. It took the chill from our tired bones. We stood so close to the burning building that our trousers and shirts were steaming visibly. Only then did we realize how hungry we were, but no food was available.

"How about a smoke?" asked the lieutenant, but we were out of cigarettes. I remembered that I had in my pocket some pipe tobacco from a store which had thrown its doors open to the public rather than permit the Germans to confiscate the merchandise. I pulled the small package from my pocket and handed it to the lieutenant.

"Any cigarette paper?" inquired the major, but silence was our response for we had none.

"Well," he smiled, "it doesn't make much difference. During the 1920 campaign I learned from our Bolshevik prisoners to roll cigarettes with newspaper—and it was possible to smoke them. Any newspaper?"

I had some and I gave it to him. We watched his fingers carefully as he rolled the first cigarette, but watching the operation and repeating it were two different things. Finally, I was able to make something vaguely resembling a cigarette even though it was crooked, of uneven thickness and virtually falling apart. I was able to smoke my creation, however, and it tasted rather well. I must say, the lieutenant's cigarette looked no better than mine.

The three of us sat down on the piles of bricks which were abundant and while the major reminisced about the war of 1920, we listened, occasionally interrupting to ask for more details. The warmth of the fire soon caused us to realize how exhausted we were, and it was with the greatest effort that we rose to our feet once more. Fortunately, the rain ended and a gentle breeze cooled our faces as we resumed our journey. Some stars appeared and the darkness seemed less intense. We had no need of them to indicate our position, however, since the rain had not extinguished the flames of burning houses in the distance. Their glow dimmer, they still served us as landmarks. We had to watch our steps in the unfamiliar terrain, especially since the ground was now slippery. It began to seem that the reddish horizon toward which we struggled, remained as remote as hours ago. There were no paths for our tired feet to follow, mud collected on our boots and our pace grew slower, heavier and more tiring. Our route wound through groves, meadows, plowed fields and wet slopes and on it were pinned all our hopes. We spoke little, only a word of caution now and then from one of us who perceived an obstacle in the darkness. I pon-

dered about my future course of action if we ever reach-
the city. Thousands upon thousands of ideas rushed
through my mind, scurrying in and out but none of
them left much impression, for I did not know what
would happen immediately, in the present, during the
next few minutes and hours. Would we reach Lvov safely or would the Germans apprehend us and perhaps kill
us?

Something moved in front of us! Something white. I
directed my rifle toward it and approached stealthily,
holding my breath as beads of cold sweat erupted on my
forehead. My finger caressed the trigger . . . advancing
carefully . . . I was ready to shoot and kill. Suddenly I
chuckled with relief when I recognized the gaze of a young
white cow whose big eyes regarded me not with fear, but
with astonishment. I brushed away the perspiration and
walked ahead.

"It is getting light. We must find a shelter. We are
probably still within the German lines," warned the
major.

"Over there" replied the lieutenant. "Houses!"

I looked in the direction of his outstretched arm and
indeed the shapes of two farmhouses could be discerned.
As we approached them cautiously, we discovered more
of them, and some modest barns. Entering one by gin-
gerly opening a massive wooden door, we checked the
inside. The barn contained two heavy peasant carts which
we used to barricade the entrance. The rest of the barn
was filled with fresh, loose, clean, fragrant, dry hay—a
sight comparable to paradise for a tired pilgrim.

As I contemplated this marvelous hay, which promised to provide me with a desirable bed and well-deserved rest, I recalled the other nights I had spent under most unusual circumstances. The first was in a railroad car, but this time it was a regular coach for transporting passengers. That time I traveled with refugees. The third, I passed in a horse-drawn cart among some sacks of grain which shifted constantly. I rode horseback during the fourth night in the middle of a moving column. During the fifth night I marched behind my horse—while holding on to his tail. When the animal stopped, I bumped against his rump and came to a halt myself. When he resumed his pace, the horse hauled me after him, still clinging to his tail with blind determination, more asleep than awake through the night. Thinking about this, I could scarcely believe it possible to march, sleep and hold on to a horse's tail all at the same time. I spent the sixth night on horseback and the seventh in the side car of a motorcycle. The next night I encountered bitter disappointment in an old farmhouse. I covered myself luxuriously with two featherbeds only to be driven from my warm nest by hundreds of bedbugs attacking me ferociously and mercilessly. I fled to a woodshed for shelter. On still another night I lay down beside my sleeping horse and enjoyed the best rest of the entire campaign. Many another night did I sleep in the motorcycle sidecar or in a horse-drawn cart. For only a few hours did I rest in a clean bed at the home of a teacher.

We crawled deep into the hay. As usual, I did not undress, but simply loosened my ammunition belt and the belt of my trousers, pointed my carbine toward the hole in the hay left by my intruding body and fell asleep at once.

I was awakened suddenly by loud voices and instinctively grabbed my carbine. But I relaxed in the next instant because the voices were Polish and one was calling my name. I scrambled out and saw a man in civilian clothes addressing my officer friends in agitation. Then I saw the joy in their faces. Seeing me come closer, the major smiled and assured me that we had made it all right, that we had almost reached the Polish urban defense lines. Polish outposts were located less than five hundred yards from us. The man in whose barn we had slept graciously invited us to breakfast and of course we would have been crazy to refuse his kind offer. While we ate he supplied us with a considerable amount of valuable information, the most important being that a few days earlier, the Soviet armies had crossed the eastern border of Poland and were approaching the city from the east. No one knew whether they were coming as friends or enemies. The Major voiced his doubts about the good intentions of the Russians. For a moment we sat in gloom then the Major stood up, ready to go and we thanked our host for his fine treat and we left his hospitable house.

"I am sorry," I said after we found ourselves alone, "but I have to return to get my horse."

"Don't!" ordered the Major. "I will be able to provide you with ten horses in Lvov."

"Thank you. I know, but I want that horse, no other!"

The officers tried to dissuade me from this risky venture since I would have to cross the German lines to reach the village where I had left the horse. The village itself was occupied by German troops. I was adamant because I felt that I could not abandon my friendly horse, leaving him to the Germans. The major and the lieutenant were soon convinced that I would not be swayed from my decision to do all in my power to reclaim my horse. They ceased theirobjections and cautioned me with expressions of concern about the dangers of my enterprise. They wished me success, luck and a safe return to the city.

I saluted them and they in return raised their hands to their caps.

As they walked away toward the Polish lines, I watched them until they disappeared among some houses on the outskirts of the suburb. I sighed and returned to the house where I had breakfast to ask the farmer for more information, assistance and advice. I realized that the effort to rescue my horse would not be easy but I also knew that it was possible and I expected to succeed.

I formulated a plan which seemed logical and feasible to me. It involved a simple deception of the Germans whom I had no desire to confront. I could not discount the possibility of being challenged by them. I reasoned that I could convince them that I was too young for service in the Polish army. In my favor was the fact that I had a fair knowledge of the German language, and this would certainly be helpful if any complications should arise. There was yet another consideration involved in my decision to retrace yesterday's arduous journey: I wanted to know what the Germans were doing. That is, I wanted information that I could put to use in a military sense. Therefore I had a "legitimate" reason for claiming my horse, for the mission would provide me an opportunity to gather certain valuable information behind enemy lines. On the other hand, I was fully aware of the dangers inherent in the situation I was about to create. However, I had high hopes, faith in myself and in the cause for which I fought.

Let's try, I thought to myself. *Nothing can happen. . .*

But if it should? whispered a faint inner voice. I listened for an answer—but none came. . .

The Polish infantry was well trained and possessed the will to defend the nation.

A LIFE FOR A HORSE

When I walked out of the barn I tried to penetrate the darkness and to reconnoiter the immediate surroundings, so that later it would not be so difficult for me to find the same barn again. I thought that I had found a solution to this problem when I heard a small waterfall near the place. I knew then that I could ask any village inhabitant to direct me to it, when necessary.

Now I retraced my steps—at considerable risk—to the same house where I had breakfast, and asked the host for assistance.

"Do you have an old civilian suit that I could get into and use?" I asked him.

"Yes," he answered after a short moment of hesitation. "What do you need it for?"

"Last night I left my horse in the nearest village about four kilometers due north from here. What is its name?"

"Why? Zboiska. But you don't want to go there! The Germans are there!"

"That's why I need the suit! I have to get my horse back!"

"Don't! It is too dangerous!"

"I have to! One doesn't leave his horse to the Germans!"

"You can be killed! Or taken prisoner!"

"I have to take that chance! Do you have the suit?"

He looked at me for a long time and I smiled at him.

He returned my smile and went out to another room. "Good"—I thought. "We understand each other."

After a short while he came back with the suit, which was rather old, black and in not too good a state of repair or cleanliness, but it was exactly what I had in mind. In these clothes I would look exactly like a young laborer, unassuming, modest—and, as I surmised, unsuspecting. I put the suit on over my uniform. I did this for two reasons, the first being that I was cold and the other, that it was not too clean. Believing in my unfailing good fortune, I entirely discarded the possibility of being caught or searched by the Germans. Nevertheless, I had to be ready to accept any future situation in which the chips could be down.

"Could you do me another favor?" I asked my helpful host.

"Now what?" he reacted impatiently.

"Here are my grenades,"—he took two steps backward—"the pistol, the rifle and my documents. If I should not return by night, please notify the nearest Polish sentry that I was probably caught by the Germans—or worse—and give him my documents also. But I am sure I'll see you before nightfall. For what I am doing, death is only a kind of a very remote possibility."

"No, sir," he answered. "It simply would be no good for me to have all those military possessions. If they were to be found by the Germans I would lose my life. If by the Poles, I could be accused of having done something to you—something bad! And remember, my house is located in no-man's land—both the Polish and German patrols have already come here! You understand."

A LIFE FOR A HORSE

I did, but what could I do with my army belongings? After a while my new friend continued.

"I know what you can do. The house next to me is empty. The family who lived there escaped to the city. A Polish soldier died there recently of wounds and was buried yesterday. Take your things there and I am certain that nobody will touch anything for nobody goes there. I will kind of watch the house, anyhow, and everything will be all right."

"Good," I said. "That's good." And I did as he suggested.

"Wish me luck!—I need it!" I told him before my departure. He made the sign of the cross and for a long time remained standing and looking in my direction.

I walked due north, not hurriedly but not too slowly either, and soon I left the last houses of the suburb coming into the fields. There was no movement on the narrow dusty village road. I quickened my pace and felt like covering the territory quickly. The morning was bright, cool and quiet, except for the occasional pounding of heavy artillery guns coming from the south and southwest from the distance of about fifteen to twenty kilometers. Around me almost all was at peace—almost, because when I sat down to relax on the green fresh grass beside the road I could perceive some isolated single rifle shots from the northeast and from time to time a bark of machine guns still farther to the east. There was no fire, whatsoever, from the north where I was going, and this very fact astonished me for a moment until I recalled that it was the German occupied sector. I stood up and resumed walking. Already the village houses were visible

behind the light morning mist when I perceived someone walking on the same road from the village in my direction, and I became instantly all eyes. A woman!—I could
scarcely believe the sight. She was moving briskly and
assuredly as if she had a firm purpose for her journey. She
looked as intently at me as I did at her when we were
coming closer. I greeted her politely without stopping and
she returned the amenity, but I noticed that she didn't
want to chat and it appeared to me as if she felt that she
was being observed from the village. I was able to ask her
the one and only question which interested me at that
moment:

"Are the Germans in the village?"

"Yes," she said without stopping. "Watch out."

I slowed down a bit, but not so much as to indicate
to any possible observer a lack of purpose in my pace. I
approached the first houses. There was no military
activity or soldiers. Soon I found myself in the middle of
the village and the road ended in a "T." Without hesitation I turned right. I had seen before approaching it that
there were more houses on my right than on the left. I
kept walking straight ahead while attempting to maintain
an appearance of purpose and trying not to turn my head
too obviously in any direction. Seeing a large house nearby, I went in and asked where in the village there was a
waterfall.

"Go on about one more kilometer in the same direction you walked," said the man. His manner of speech
was apprehensive and so were his eyes. His direct answer
gave me proof that the man saw me before I entered his
house. He must have observed the road through the win-

dows. I thanked him for the directions and I left.

The village street was wide, but there was no one on it except me. I had an uncanny feeling of being observed from houses I was passing. Then in the distance I saw a column of soldiers marching in my direction. German soldiers! With their helmets looking like robot heads, they seemed unreal to me. During the past weeks I was constantly shooting at their likes, maybe at these very soldiers! My right hand went automatically for my pistol, only to find that it was not there. I stepped to the side to let the soldiers pass without being too close to them, and I eyed them with considerable interest, trying to look as unconcerned as possible. Some of them returned a tired gaze. Indeed, they had to be tired, if only for the burdens they carried on their shoulders: rifles, submachine guns, light machine guns and parts of heavy ones, ammunition in large boxes and loose ammunition belts, gas masks, food rations, rolled blankets, eating utensils, packs with underwear, socks and toiletries, coats and camouflage materials, parts of suits—well, all that soldiers need. I suddenly remembered that these were the units who, in fighting us, had lost all their transport vehicles, armoured cars and tanks!

Their column passed; there came another group. Polish soldiers taken prisoner, now serving their captors as animals of burden. They also were carrying on their shoulders heavy packs and boxes which I recognized as ammunition boxes.

"Well"—I thought bitterly, "against all international conventions, including that of Geneva, they are using prisoners in the war effort against their own country!'' As the prisoners were passing some looked at me with searching eyes. They probably noticed my heavy military boots and wondered about my identity. I kept walking slowly all the time as they passed by. Their German guards didn't pay any attention to me, because they were busy urging the prisoners to walk faster and shouting at them the expedient Polish "dali", a perverted form of "dalej" which means "go on"! The prisoners' column was long and I was afraid that my face might betray my feelings. I tried carefully to control the muscles of my face. I was relieved only when the prisoners finally passed and I had the street again all to myself. I moved faster as I attempted again to assume an air of being busy.

Soon I heard the waterfall and with no difficulty at all, I found the farm I was looking for. I turned sharply to my left toward it and in no time, was inside. Hurrah!— my black beauty stood quietly in the far left corner of the stable, his color contrasting sharply with the white-washed walls. I became even more elated when I found the saddle and my sabre attached to it. Then I looked at two white cows with reddish spots and I chuckled remembering last night when in darkness I entered the barn with great precaution and suddenly heard heavy breathing, without knowing who was breathing so loudly and became scared until I smelled the cow.

A shadow passed on my right and I turned my head instantly. An old man and a young girl stood at the door. I greeted them and explained the situation.

"Oh, I see, I see"—repeated the man—"and I wondered whose horse it might be! And some German soldiers must have done the same, for in the early morning they searched the premises, looked at your horse, found the saddle and even took a leather strap..." While the man continued to describe this event in detail I checked the leather harness and, of course, there was lacking only one single piece of leather, the so-called breast strap, which led from around the neck between the front legs, then under the breast to hold the main strap of the saddle at the belly, thus to prevent it from sliding backward and to assure the saddle's steadiness during the ride. I knew that the missing strap would not prevent me from riding and I saddled the horse at once.

"What do you think to do, sir?"—asked the old man.

"To take my horse to Lvov, of course," I smiled. "Where else?"

"Will you make it? You have to cross the German lines!"

"I already did it once, at night. It will be easier the second time, in daylight!"

"Maybe it will be easier for you and safer to wait here? The Germans seem to be vacating our village and going back west." I became all attention:

"Are you sure?"

"Well, I saw no movement toward the east."

I pondered for awhile, but the decision was difficult. I had two choices. One involved the risks of a short, but dangerous journey through enemy positions. The other promised a more peaceful waiting for development of events. But it was just this waiting in German occupied territory that made me ill at ease, for I had not even one personal document on my person which would prove my identity in case of need. Further, I was concerned about being inactive in the village. I was needed in the city as one of its defenders. In addition, I felt uncomfortable in an unknown locality, the more so as I knew it was inhabited not only by the Poles, but by the German-friendly, misguided Ukrainians. Last, but not least, I was disturbed by the immediate future of the village in case of German withdrawal and nagged by a self-imposed question as to who in town would be the lord and master of the community—the oncoming Russians, or the Ukrainians? Or, perhaps, a village militia or guards would take over from the Germans? However, the most important reason to totally reject waiting it out was my feeling of the basic soldier's duty: to join his fighting unit— any fighting unit still resisting the enemy.

My decision made, I told the old man, who only shook his head, asked me whether I was hungry and offered me some apples. I tasted one at once. They were sweet and mellow and I took so many of them that my pockets were bulging. I shook hands with the girl and her father, led my horse to the street and mounted quickly.

Riding east I observed my immediate surroundings carefully, without turning my head, endeavoring again to pass for a casual rider on one of the countless daily routines of peasant life.

A moment later I went into high alertness. I saw another marching unit of the German soldiers, mixed with Polish prisoners-of-war, the latter carrying ammunition boxes. They were walking in the opposite direction to mine. When we approached each other I held my horse to the side of the road, took some apples out of my pocket and stretched them invitingly to the passing soldiers. None of them took any. One German private walking rather slowly had time to tell me as he passed, "Nichts gut. Cholera!" I gave him a friendly smile as answer.

About two hundred meters behind the column I saw some dozen of Germans busily winding up the telephone cables upon drums they carried. "God be praised"—I rejoiced quietly. "They are really going away." It was the best proof that they were departing.

So far I was lucky. I was not accosted by any German in spite of the fact that an army saber was visibly attached to my saddle. I would have felt like a traitor if I had left my saber behind. I soon reached the end of the village near a small, but thick grove to the south, i.e. to my right. I heard short repeated series of a heavy machine gunfire, which must have been directed away from me, because I didn't hear any bullets. "It must be a German rear guard marking the presence of an army unit," I said to myself. In order not to take any unnecessary chances I abandoned the hard surface of the road, changing direction to due north. Only after laying considerable distance between myself and the machine gun did I dare to return to my easterly course, having circled around the point of danger. There were some shots from the southwesterly direction, but the firing was remote and harmless.

It was afternoon before I stumbled upon a wide, hard-surface highway that ran from north-northeast to south-southwest. It had to lead straight to Lvov. I turned my horse in the new direction holding to the very edge of the road along a deep rainwater ditch, now dry. I rode on the soft soil to avoid the clang of the horseshoes which would prevent me from hearing the noises of war. An almost perfect calm reigned around us and only from the southwest came the far, deep din of artillery. There was not a living soul moving on the roadway. It was straight as an arrow, empty as a grave and made me shudder. I felt strangely disquieted, full of unexplained foreboding. On this warm, almost hot afternoon, a cold shiver ran down my spine—the angel of death suddenly flying past!

"I must be tired"—I thought. To disperse the mood I spurred my horse into a quick trot. The next large road crossing carried a road sign with the inscription: "Lvov—7 km". It made me more alert. These were the final kilometers separating me from the safety of the unyielding bastion of the Polish southeastern territories. I rode fast. Only a few minutes later another sign read "4 km". Shortly afterward, having passed over the crest of a gently rolling hill, I saw the tall church steeples of the city and I rejoiced! I was coming home to my family, friends, meadows and woods.

All of a sudden I was hit hard by the indescribably offensive smell which I knew so well—the stink of death. My horse refused to proceed. When I urged him on he balked, turned, and tried to run away into the field. I dismounted holding the reins lightly and gripped his halter, leading him to overcome his resistance. His head hung low, his ears betrayed his anxiety by their quick movements, a thick foam from his mouth was falling on the ground. He started to groan as if in pain, and I perceived that he was shivering. I searched the ground visually but I did not see any decomposing corpses. The stench was becoming stronger and so much more unbearable that I had to put a handkerchief to my nose. Then... what a horrifying sight! In the deep drainage ditch at the roadside were a row of bodies lying close to each other— all still—no movement—no sound...I came closer searching for signs of life in any of them. Then I saw their faces ...all grey...and some black. I crossed the road to the other ditch. The same sight. Dead soldiers in Polish uniforms...all young...all in the same position with heads low and legs bent at the knees. There were horrible wounds in their heads, breasts and bellies. Some bodies were ripped apart by large caliber bullets. It was horrible.

Attempting to recreate the situation and the cause of this tragedy, I found an explanation. The Germans must have placed some heavy machine guns further north and directed them into the ditches. The first must have been deadly accurate during the Polish night attack. It could have happened only at night, when in the darkness the first soldier moving in the ditch must have been hit without the second soldier noticing it. Then in almost the same second the next soldier was killed and the next and so on. The difference in time from the first to the last soldier at the very end of the file must have been only seconds—not even a minute. The ditches were the only approach to the German lines from the Lvov defense perimeter. All the country around was as flat as a plate and devoid of any protective growth whatsoever. The person or persons responsible for the more than three hundred deaths, I concluded, was whoever suggested the ditches as an approach route for the attacking Polish soldiers. I walked near the ditch on my left, holding the horse's canter in my right hand, mourning for those lives spent uselessly. Someone made a mistake in judgment...and there seemed to be no end to the long row of the dead.

I became violently sick, but kept walking toward some suburban houses. I noticed some moving shapes in one ditch. Coming closer I saw about half a dozen boys aged from twelve to fourteen, searching the pockets of the dead soldiers and taking valuables from the corpses.

"Do you know," I tried to scare them, "that robbing dead soldiers carries an instant death penalty?"

"On your way, soldier!" barked one of them, "or you can get hurt!" He waved a heavy military Mauser pistol in his right hand, menacing me. To argue with this young hyena would be inviting trouble. I had no weapon except the saber, and a bullet is a bit faster than a saber. The children went on with their infamous procedure, and I walked slowly away resolving to notify the military authorities at once about the need to bury the dead.

In less than one kilometer, I came to a road barricade. I approached slowly, knowing full well that it must surely be manned by the Poles. As I came close to the barricade I noticed that it was very hastily thrown together. An overturned streetcar was the main impediment around which pieces of timber and old furniture were heaped haphazardly. It was all placed on the edge of a large and deep concrete lined ditch. In the middle of the ditch flowed a small stream—the "Peltev"—I recalled the name of the little river. As I thought about crossing it, I was hailed in Polish.

"Halt!"—A strong voice called out. "Who goes there?"

"A Polish soldier! Don't shoot! I come from the German lines!"

Silence for a moment and then a command: "Lay down your weapons and cross with your hands up!"

"I don't have any arms!" I shouted back. "I have only a horse! How can I cross with the horse?"

"Tie it firmly to anything you can and come over with your hands up!"

"All right! Just a minute!"

I walked around the edge of the barricade and tied the reins of my horse around a heavy, long wooden beam. With my hands half up, I skidded down the steep, slippery bank of the stream. I crossed it dry on a wooden board with ease. The stream was only four or five yards wide. As I climbed the opposite bank, soldiers in grass green uniforms pulled me up. I saluted them smartly and they returned my military greeting. I smiled my happiest smile at them and they grinned back.

I felt good. Very good indeed! Being tired, dusty and hungry didn't matter. It was good to be among friends, among fellow soldiers! They stood there eyeing me with curiosity. I kept smiling silently, still thinking with pride of my recent accomplishment of recovering my horse from the German-held village and making it safely back to the city to help in its defense.

"Can you give me a cigarette?" I asked them. "I don't have any!"

"Please help yourself!" An open package was extended to me.

I took a cigarette and felt still better.

BECOMING A "GERMAN SPY"

It felt good to be back in Lvov.

I had returned to my own people whom I needed so much and to the organized fighting force which refused to be defeated—in the city that stands well up among all Polish cities—*Leopolis semper fidelis*, "Lvov always faithful."

Having obliged me with a cigarette, the soldiers reported my arrival from a German-occupied village to their company command through a green field telephone. The non-commissioned officer in charge of the unit informed me that the company commander would like to see me at once and that I should prepare a detailed report concerning my observations behind enemy lines. Since I had interesting and important information to disclose I thought it best to go immediately. I asked for directions to company headquarters, but was told that it would be impossible for me to locate the well-camouflaged unit command without help. A soldier was directed to accompany me to my destination. I saluted everybody and thanked them for their hospitality and the cigarettes which I had smoked freely while chatting. I left with a feeling of urgency. I had certain intelligence for the Poles that seemed vital. The private who walked with me gave the impression of an amiable young soldier. He talked and joked about the Germans, the war situation in general, the landing of French and British troops in Rumania from whence allied military transports were already rolling to our relief, about the Red Army which had crossed the eastern border of Poland to assist us against the Germans, and so forth. We talked in a friendly manner during our walk. The road was long and circuitous. We had to dodge tank impediments, ditches and open spaces which afforded no protection from the inevitable German gunfire which seemed to burst with continuous strength from the north and west in spite of the lateness of the afternoon. Entering a deep ditch and making a few turns, we reached our destination.

My companion reported his arrival to the assistant commanding officer as did I, whereupon I was taken immediately to the commander, a captain. I delivered my report to him in the presence of other officers, describing in the minutest detail what I had seen behind German lines, without omitting even the slightest or seemingly most trivial items which had any remote connection with military matters. I was required to answer many questions and I began to grow tired. Slowly, I became aware of an almost imperceptible mood of incredulity in my interrogators which grew more obvious as the debriefing continued. Their attitude made me angry enough to ridicule some questions which were hurled at me impolitely.

In the past I had sometimes regretted my hostile response toward people who displayed rudeness, prejudice or lack of good manners toward me. Nevertheless, to this day I am unable to refrain from making certain assumptions about the person who treats me unjustly or negatively, condemning me without a hearing or trial or even an attempt at simple human understanding. There is no justice without mercy, and it is this combination which I seek from humans in all relationships. Thus it was that my reactions to an illogical and inexplicable hostility toward me by my fellow officers had to bring me into difficulties.

"You are under arrest as a German spy!" exclaimed the captain who must have had enough of my ridicule.

"You are idiots!" I shouted back at him and his company.

"Take him at once to the battalion commander!" he ordered in a high-pitched voice. "And out with him! I don't talk to spies—I shoot them!"

The sergeant-major, a middle-aged man, provided me with an escort of his soldiers who, according to regulations, affixed their bayonets to their rifles. Then he recited a solemn formula that I would be shot without warning if I tried to escape. In reply I laughed in his face and spat disgustedly at his feet. He ordered me to step back and averted his face.

It was anything but easy for me to walk between the two bared bayonets, the more so because our route brought us into contact with many passersby. They asked the soldiers who I was and received the curt answer: "A German spy." I was a likely candidate for a lynching on several occasions and only the assurances of my guards about the certainty of military justice which awaited me kept my would-be oppressors from laying hands on me. If ever in my life I had experienced long hours or long roads, this was certainly an example of both. With clenched teeth I cursed the criminal stupidity of the paranoid company commander, berating also his lack of psychological insight which had caused this inexcusable misunderstanding. I lamented my own role in the situation because I was forced to bear the brunt of his ineptness. I also reflected on the wasted time and effort of all those concerned in this farce and wondered how many others would soon become involved. I began to experience some misgivings since the possibility grew that this little tragi-comedy might turn into a full tragedy. Things appeared much less bright than I might have wished. My thoughts were interrupted by our arrival in the courtyard of a three-story house. Traffic was heavy in the area and it appeared to be the headquarters of battalion command. Numerous soldiers, officers and military vehicles were in evidence.

Fortunately, the higher brass was brief and precise about hearing my report which I repeated in exactly the same way that I had already delivered the information. They responded by sending me immediately to the supreme command of the city, an organization tantamount to army headquarters.

The most important information I reported concerned the German retreat from the village of Zboiska. I was told that this vital bit of tactical news would have to be verified. If investigation confirmed my statement, I was to receive a medal, but if the Polish patrols sent to Zboiska should be attacked or destroyed, I might expect to suffer the consequences. Carrying no identification papers I was informed that the address of my family was being checked, an easy matter to dispose of. To await the outcome of all these verifications, I was led to a large guard room. All the doors and windows were open. I was treated to a cup of coffee, cookies and cigarettes. I noted that my guards had removed the bayonets from their rifles and become a shade friendlier. However, after the treatment they had given me I preferred not to look at them and turned my back on them.

At that point a lucky incident came to my rescue. There was a loud shout: "Robert! What are you doing here?"

I turned around—and what good luck! It was John Katchen, one of my best friends from the soccer team, approaching me with concern evident on his alert face, for he saw me under guard, dressed in a shabby outfit with my face looking a good bit less than its best. John, on the contrary, wore the immaculately clean uniform of a cadet-officer and looked a paragon of young manhood. He identified himself quickly to the guards, listened to their story briefly then walked briskly away after assuring me: "Don't worry! I am going straight to army staff premises. I will take care of everything. And how!"

He was gone. I had not been permitted to speak with him, but I took heart because I realized that "lady luck", the most unpredictable ally of all, the most whimsical and unreliable comrade had returned to my side!

In a few minutes, John reappeared all smiles, and a moment later my maternal grand uncle came running toward me, out of breath and carrying some sandwiches and a thermos of hot chocolate. He was a former high official of the provisional government who still retained a considerable amount of influence in the city. He was all ears about my adventure which John had related to him in the form released by headquarters. When I had devoured all of the food at hand, I asked for more and John went to seek some more substantial fare. In his absence I supplied my uncle with additional details to fill in the gaps in John's narration about me.

Half an hour later the general's aide-de-camp entered the guard room to direct me to the operations room. My guards started to follow us, but he stopped them with an impatient movement of his hand and ordered them to report back to their own unit. I walked with him to an office on the second floor where he handed me a sheet of paper. I read it and blushed up to my ears. It was a citation for bravery and extraordinary performance of duty.

"It will be printed in the army's daily orders day after tomorrow," he said. "I thank you for all you have done. It was an excellent job. Good-bye." I saluted and left. I said a quick "so long" to John and my uncle and promised to see them soon.

Evening was approaching and the sun's rays were fading, but there was sufficient light to run fast to the northern suburb where I had hidden my arms and documents before crossing the German Front lines on my way to Zboiska. I located the house with ease and it felt good to get rid of the old suit and return it to the man who had loaned it to me, but it felt superb to feel my pistol and rifle once more on my person.

I hurried to the post where my horse was waiting. To shorten the route, I chose to move along the defense perimeter. In this way I expected to encounter very little traffic since the line was virtually deserted at that time.

BECOMING A "GERMAN SPY"

My strategy was good, but the Germans unexpectedly opened fire at an important crossroads forcing me to swerve away from the direct route and circle around through a large empty farm where tomatoes had been cultivated. There I found some manned outposts which had recently been shelled by German artillery. Steadily, but with caution, I advanced avoiding both heavy machine gun fire and sporadic artillery coming from the northwest. Near one of the barricades I saw a young boy vainly attempting to lead a splendid horse away from the line of fire. The boy was small and weak and his strength was no match for the large horse who refused to move. I rushed over and within a minute both horse and boy were safe behind the barricade. I noticed a very small hole at the side of the horse's belly. It was a bullet hole which did not even bleed. I was powerless to help the animal and could only hope that the wound was not serious and that the bullet had done no extensive damage to his intestines.

I neared the spot where I had left my horse. Skirting an orchard I saw him standing patiently, awaiting my return. The soldiers from the post did not recognize me at first for they had not expected to see me in uniform. They rejoiced later when I recounted my recent adventures. They boasted about feeding my horse while I was away. I thanked them verbally and with cigarettes which John had provided.

A moment later I was riding toward the heart of the city. Tired, but in a happy frame of mind, my fatigue did not seem oppressive. It grew dark, but the surface of the road was still distinguishable by the silhouettes of houses. I moved without difficulty. I was nearly asleep in the saddle when my horse neighed, bringing back full consciousness. Where was I? In front of an army barracks. I dismounted, went inside, reported and returned to the courtyard filled with straw. Unsaddling my horse, I tied him securely to a fence and buried myself deeply in the warm straw. I did not even know when I fell asleep.

BESIEGED

Just before midnight I awakened from the heavy sleep feeling fresh and alert despite its brevity. I dug out from under the thick layer of straw which had kept me warm, cleaned up, got my horse ready, and rode out of the military barracks. Was it the constant and incessant noise, the endless coming and going of soldiers and vehicles which had awakened me?

I shrugged my shoulders and mentally switched gears. Now it would take all my mental faculties to reach my uncle's stables at the opposite end of the city. The darkness of the night, the siege, the martial law imposed upon the fortress—all weighed upon my mind. I wanted to avoid any unpleasant situations that could be prevented.

Quiet reigned all around. I discounted the far din of artillery coming from the west and south. The hooves of my horse were sharply audible on the hard surface of the side street which I had taken deliberately. I didn't have a pass, and I assumed they were required for army personnel moving around the city under siege. As if in answer to the thought, I was hailed by an unseen guard! He stood in a building doorway. Fortunately I was able to give him the password, and explained my situation quickly. That seemed to convince him. As I pulled away he stepped out from his vantage point together with two other soldiers who held rifles at the ready. I saluted them.

They wished me luck, simultaneously warning me about the possibility of ambushes by the German fifth column and saboteurs. As a precaution I opened my gun holster to have my Mauser handy within a split second. Military patrols checked me twice more before I arrived at the large apartment house in which my uncle lived with his family. His neighbors told me that the building's occupants had moved into the cellar out of fear of artillery shelling and air bombardment.

I descended a steep dimly-lit staircase that led to huge underground halls full of people. My eyes bulged at the sight of the activity, noise and excitement. Women, old men, and children who disregarded the late hour—it was well past midnight—were acting as though it were broad daylight.

Some women were cooking food on portable kerosene or spirit stoves; others tried vainly to keep a watch over the children. They seemed to be all over the place, running, playing, shouting, and ignoring the remonstrations and pleadings of the old men and some young girls who were running after those kids like old roosters and young hens. Beds and collapsible cots stood in lines along the walls of the shelter, whose space appeared to be organized with the utmost economy and with consideration for passages connecting individual rooms. Uncounted chests and boxes full of kitchen utensils, blankets, pieces of bedding, and a thousand-and-one items of daily usage were placed near the beds and served as tables and chairs. I stood in a broad passageway between two rooms, close to the wall, a good point for observing the scene around me. My uniform aroused no attention.

BESIEGED

Other soldiers came in, ate quickly and left. Two privates were sleeping in the corner in the midst of all the racket. How well I understood their fatigue which defied the surrounding uproar for the sake of gaining a bit of rest under any conditions.

I stood there observing and listening as well as I could to the loud conversations of the adults, following the sudden changes of direction of scampering children playing cops and robbers, or others busying themselves with the game of hide-and-seek —for which these surroundings were perfect. I reflected for a moment on the contrast between the carefree children's play and the bitter reality of the war outside. I had to move on to find my relatives, to feed my horse, and to go to bed—if I were able to find one—but I was so fascinated with the unreal world unfolding before my eyes that I remained standing rooted to the floor. I looked for a long time at life where there was no shooting and killing. My watch read three o'clock when I decided with regret that I had to go on.

It took only a few minutes to find my aunt and cousins in one of the adjacent rooms. She greeted me in an unusually distracted manner and at once started to complain about the war and everything connected with it. She did such a good job of lamenting that I started to feel guilty about the war myself, as if I carried some responsibility for its being forced on Poland. She made me angry with her incessant grumbling, but I kept cool. My cousins began making signs behind her back. After a while she caught herself, stopped whining, and even regained enough composure to invite me to have a bite. I refused, firmly excusing myself on the grounds of being occupied with military duties. I left her in an almost abrupt manner, asking her, however, to pay my respects to all of her family.

Without incident I found my uncle's stable, and it was good to greet my uncle there, who preferred the company of his horses to that of his wife. I didn't blame him in the least. Two of my cousins slept in his guest room while my uncle and his stable men kept busy grooming and tending his magnificent animals, among them some of the finest racing stock in Poland. Breeding them had become not only his hobby but also the source of a considerable income, as he exported many of the studs and mares. I placed my gelding in his care and went to bed without losing a minute.

At about nine o'clock in the morning I woke up feeling that someone was in my room. I was right. My younger cousins greeted me with obvious signs of admiration (I thought to myself it was for my uniform and weapons). They made themselves helpful in whatever I was doing. I quickly made my morning toilette, especially enjoying a shower, after which I felt rather good. Off I went to volunteer my services to the army distribution point. There, unexpectedly, I was informed that I had two days of leave coming by order of the H.Q. to which I was to report directly after the elapse of that time. Well, since the army was not aching for my presence, it occurred to me that I could visit all my relatives, of whom there were five families, all on my mother's side. But first I had to return to the stables to talk with my uncle, whom

I had missed in the late morning when I got up. I surmised that he might be the most knowledgeable person among my relatives, so I rode back to his stables and this time I was lucky, for when I entered his offices I saw him sitting behind his desk writing.

"Ah, here you are," he greeted me. "Sit down and tell me all about your doings."

"Well, there is not too much to tell that you don't already know," I answered, "but I would like to ask you some questions about the general situation, as I have been completely cut off from any reliable information about the war."

"The news is not good at all," he answered gravely. "The Red Army is approaching the city from the east and disarming our units. There were a few skirmishes reported in the process. Our government has crossed the border into Rumania. Warsaw and Pomerania are resisting the Germans. Some heavy fighting is going on there. . ."

"What about Lvov? What will happen here?"

"No one is certain whether it will resist the Soviets or not. It was quite successful against the Germans, but to handle them both at the same time...I don't know. Oh, by the way, do you know that the Ukrainian nationalists within the city have been serving the Germans all the time? And that they did fifth-column work for the Nazis? Many small Polish army units retreating east before the Germans were ambushed and annihilated by them. We have the word that they act like hosts for the Germans in some of the Nazi-occupied regions of Poland...And another matter: German authorities have notified the

Ukrainian leaders to move west of the San and Bug rivers. East of that line is to be Soviet territory. We received that news from several Ukrainian sources friendly to us, to whom it was leaked from their higher-ups. This is confirmed. Many highly placed Ukrainians and their community leaders have packed up in a hurry and gone west to join the Germans. . ."

"Many of these events took place outside of Lvov," I interjected, "so how is it possible for you to know about all this?"

"The city was never hermetically sealed, as you know yourself. You were able to cross the front lines three times in about twelve hours. But there really were no front lines as such, only strongholds situated very close to each other. Of course, a group of soldiers or civilians could have passed unnoticed to either side. Do I answer your criticism?"

"Naturally, naturally," I reassured him quickly, "but it was not meant as a critical remark. I only want to know more details. Forgive me, please, for this distraction." My uncle nodded acquiesence, a faint gentle smile on his face, while I continued my questions quickly.

"Where is the whole Polish armed force? Destroyed? Taken prisoner? Gone to Rumania? What are we to do? Is the whole of Poland already in the hands of our enemies?

"I am afraid so. About 10 percent of the military has been annihilated, 20 percent are prisoners, 10-15 percent escaped to Rumania and Hungary, and I believe also to Lithuania and Latvia, while the rest—and it is a high number, between 55 and 60 percent—is still resisting, or donning civilian clothing in which to reach their homes. Many soldiers are hiding in cities, towns, villages and hamlets, forests and woods. Some of them have repeatedly interrupted the German lines of communication. I hope that the majority of the 60 percent will get home safely. You see, this is my opinion at which I arrived on the basis of all the material that was available to me at army headquarters, where I am still serving as civilian adviser. . .''

A hush fell upon us and it became so disquietingly long I was literally able to hear a fly buzzing aimlessly at the window pane trying to go through it into the free air. *Poor fly and poor us,* I thought, and without realizing what I was doing I stood up, opened the window and let the fly out.

"I am sorry, it made me nervous," I lied, blushing, because I was certain that he knew why I let the fly escape and that I was lying. I looked out the window without seeing anything. My thoughts were in turmoil. I could not comprehend the fact that a country, a state, a nation, *my nation*, was falling prey to assassins. I was still at the window looking with unseeing eyes, when my uncle broke the silence.

"What do you intend to do?"

"I will go to the citadel. The armory is there and I need a good gun if I can find one. You see," I pointed to my army issue carbine, "this is not even a semi-automatic weapon and in these times and situation I'll need something. The city seems to be one of the last points of struggle and I would not like to be killed as one of the last victims. . .I want to get out of this war alive. . .''

"I don't blame you at all," he smiled at me.

"So long then, Uncle!" I saluted him smartly. He rose from his chair and embraced me warmly.

"Should you ever need something, anything, you know where to find me." I was deeply moved and left quickly.

From Upper Yanovska street I went across to Grodecka near St. Elizabeth Church and down Sapiehy. My mood of despair at the fall of the Polish nation did not last long, because this time history came to me as a solace, and I recalled to mind the first bloody downfall of the Polish Empire that extended then from the Danube to the Baltic Sea, and from the Elbe to Dnieper, and its circumstances in 1032; and the feudal disintegration in the 13th century, the epoch of the Fire and Sword; the Deluge in the 17th century so vividly described by Sienkiewicz, who wrote to uplift men's hearts; and the first partition of the splendid multi-lingual, religious and national Empire in 1772, the second in 1793 and the final one in 1795. One of the few democracies in Europe, Poland went down under the totalitarian attack of the henchmen of Russia, Prussia and Austria. Those henchmen existed and grew by reason of Polish benevolence, extended to them with never a suspicion that these countries would later repay their debt of gratitude to Poland in the most nefarious, hypocritical and murderous way. They tore her apart like international vultures. Even their national emblems, black eagles, reminded one of vultures! Then they declared themselves the Holy Alliance (it was anything but that). The true nature of that alliance was exposed clearly during the First World War, when their armies fell upon each other. (I didn't know then that another similar

children or adolescents got hold of a rifle or pistol and were "playing" with it. Suddenly I was stunned by a long machine gun salvo coming from very close, about two hundred yards to my right, somewhere in the side streets. The firing ceased as abruptly as it began. Passersby started to run into the nearest house doors. I felt naked riding in the middle of the street, so I swung my rifle from my shoulders to my chest and let it hang there.

Soon I arrived at the house of my other uncle, a printing shop owner, but nobody was at home so I continued to ride toward the armory. This time, as a precaution, I kept the horse on the right side of the street and carefully observed everything around me. I didn't see anything suspicious. Then a man in a military uniform appeared coming from the opposite direction. He practically ran toward me and I halted my horse. His uniform was that of an officer, but his epaulets were gone, and I looked at him with astonishment, for I had never seen a soldier without epaulets...and an officer?

"Throw your rifle down!" he said excitedly. "The Ukrainians are disarming Polish soldiers! Get rid of your pistol and grenades! Lvov has just surrendered to the Soviets. The city is now in nobody's hands. The mob is taking over! Save yourself!"

I became angry and indignant, and I spoke with disdain:

"How could you, a Polish officer let *anyone* disarm you?"

He looked at me with widening eyes, shook his head in disbelief, made a desperate movement with his hand, signifying that I was in his interpretation a hopeless case—and he was gone without uttering another word. I brought the rifle to the ready and became sharply alert—but there was nothing unusual about the street with only a few men on it.

Now, I thought, *the crucial moment has come. I must reach the citadel in a hurry,* and I was elated, for only a kilometer or so separated me from it. I put my horse into a trot. Within ten minutes we entered the large courtyard of the stronghold. The guard at the gate stood there talking with other soldiers and didn't ask me any questions, giving me only a cursory glance. Some soldiers had their rifles on, others did not. I rode to the nearest building, asked for the commanding officer's whereabouts and was shown the way by a soldier. I knocked at the door but there was no answer. I opened it and entered. I found myself in a large room with office desks and chairs and the walls plastered with all kinds of maps with numerous markings on them. A group of a dozen or more officers was engaged in an animated conversation, but I must have made quite an entrance, for all heads turned to me and a moment of silence ensued. I reasoned that it must have been my battle-ready outfit that stunned them, because for the past few hours I had not seen a single soldier in the heart of the city who was wearing all his battle paraphernalia. I had a helmet on my head with a strap around my chin, a rifle hung on my right soldier, a pistol in a large holster was at my hip, and four hand grenades were attached to my belt. Approaching the group I noticed that the highest ranking officer was a lieutenant colonel.

BESIEGED

"Colonel, sir. Cadet officer Vansword reports his arrival and asks for orders!" I recited the formula of arrival.

I stood there in front of them, looking into their faces, and felt all eyes directed toward me. I will never forget that moment. They were looking at me with such an expression of gentleness, friendship and fondness, that it embarrassed me in a most touching and pleasant manner. The thought shot through my mind like lightning that they must have seen in me a very young man who refused to give up in the face of adversity, in the face of the end. In this instant I felt with the strongest emotion that we were all brothers and sons of our great mother—Poland.

The officer to whom I reported stood up and came to me slowly, with steady steps, and stopped directly before me. Standing before him at attention in the best military posture, I saw in grim detail the fine features of his face. His kind eyes seemed to be covered with a film of moisture, or was it my own?

"Our army has ceased to exist," he began. My heart beat faster. "We have surrendered to the Red Army. Poland is occupied by the Germans and the Soviets." Little drops of sweat appeared on my forehead. Silence fell over the room. "The siege of Lvov is over!"

So, that is it, I thought.

Now my aunt's complaints could cease, she could move out of the cellar and return to her apartment on the second floor, the floor of the elite in European cities. There would be no more shooting. We had lost the war . . . what would happen next?

All these thoughts jumbled through my brain, a shudder ran down my spin. The lieutenant colonel was still standing in front of us. His eyes became sad. He extended his hand and shook mine.

"Thank you for your services," he said.

"For the glory of the fatherland," was my routine answer. Another beautiful-sounding military patriotic formula that came out automatically instead of a senseless, "thank you."

So, that is it, came repeatedly to my mind. It buzzed in my ears like an echoing drone. There was no escape. It had to be lived with, no matter how difficult.

Other questions, other doubts and uncertainties began to bother me. Are we to become prisoners of war? Will we simply be permitted to go home? Was there a way out? Was there anything we could do?

Calm down, calm down, I kept repeating to myself. Think. Think it through. Slowly, calmly!Perhaps there is something to be done—! Try to think. Try harder—to think—think—my God!

A CITY IN SURRENDER

The colonel's news about the surrender of the city and of the army group hit me hard. Realizing finally that there was nothing for me to do there anymore, I saluted him and turned to leave the commander's room. The other officers came to me and there ensued one of those conversations full of questions, advice, doubts, counsels, possibilities, plans and limitations.

"When did you eat last?" a Major asked.

"Thanks. I couldn't eat now," was my answer.

"Well, how about a glass of wine? You are over eighteen, aren't you?"

"Yes. Thank you. With pleasure."

He brought me a glass of red wine which tasted delicious.

"I assume that you want to go home. Please be careful and do not leave the citadel before darkness falls. If you prefer to keep your arms, be aware of the risks involved. The Ukrainians are disarming our soldiers and they are not to be trusted. Above all, get rid of your uniform. Don't worry about food, because we have already opened our stores to the civilian population and everybody who wants something can take whatever is available. You can help yourself to some, too."

His suggestions were timely. I thanked him and left quickly to get the necessary food for a few days journey. I had to cover about seventy miles from Lvov to my home town of Przemysl. The major was right about the accessibility of the military food supplies. Numerous persons, some soldiers, the majority civilians, were carrying armsful of food away with them. It was a good decision to open the government stores to the public so that the armies of a foreign power would not get the booty of food, needed so badly by the people. Some canned meat attached itself to me and soon my two large saddlebags were filled with it. I took a large sack of other meats which I could not have carried very far, but it was for the third branch of my family which lived just three hundred yards from the citadel.

I decided to put some other clothing over my uniform. Upon entering the rooms full of military apparel, my attention focused upon the warm but light army equipment which could pass in an emergency for quasi-civilian and quasi-military attire. Fortune was with me. A warm woolen sweater and heavy duty trousers I found were my size.

This was the first time in my life, I reflected, that I got something without paying for it. On second thought, I decided soberly, I would gladly return all those goodies if only Poland came back into existence.

It was getting dark when I rode out of the stronghold. Two minutes later I was with Uncle Ted's family. His apartment was large, because he had four sons, three daughters and, of course, a wife. They could well have used a little more living space for nine persons. Nevertheless he invited me at once to stay and to continue my trip back home after the situation clarified itself enough to permit safe travel. His suggestion tempted me, but I had to give priority to reaching my mother and my brother. I said "so long" and was on my way.

Once outside, I understood his misgivings about my journey. There was constant rifle fire at irregular intervals, scattered, single shots, but persistent, at various distances all around. The streets were empty and the clear night provided good visibility. It grew still better when I reached Sapiehy Street, a wide spacious boulevard lined with trees. My horse was stepping lightly, but the sound of his shoes could be heard for a good distance. This fact did nothing to cheer me, because my coming was being announced to anyone who lay in wait. Fortunately, everyone in the whole peaceless city seemed to be minding other business.

I was moving toward Grodecka Street, the main artery straight west to Grodek and Przemysl. Close to St. Elizabeth Church, directed lights from behind the trees and nearby houses flashed on, blinding me. A hoarse voice gave a sharp command to halt. I covered my eyes with my left hand and reined my mount to a stop.

"Who are you?" asked the voice.

"A civilian going home!"

"Dismount and identify yourself!"

As I did I could detect some people coming closer. In the light of their own flashlights I counted seven. *Not a chance to fight them* crossed my mind. My rifle was on my back, the pistol holster was closed. *Not a chance. . . but why fight them? Maybe they will let me go?*

Their red armbands came into full view while they examined my documents. They stood around me, asked questions about me and my family. They wanted to know who I was and where my allegiance belonged. I had to answer their questions. The red militiamen were tough.

"We have to take you to our commissar" said the hoarse-voiced leader. "Follow me and don't try to do anything foolish, or else. . ."

The whole patrol accompanied me. We walked five hundred yards to Szeptycki Street, where we entered a house and went up to the second floor. On my way I noted the lack of efficiency of this patrol that caught me. They had left their post unmanned and uncontrolled. Anybody could pass through that point in the meantime. I hoped prayerfully that other soldiers like myself were slipping through that very spot to their freedom.

Here is my bad luck again I thought, passing through a nice hall and entering the large, well-furnished office of the commissar.

The patrol commander reported my presence in a leisurely manner to a man in a dark suit, about thirty-five years old, sitting at a table. His facial features were sharp with a Semitic nose, protruding ears, dark eyes and eyebrows. He had the air of an intellectual and gave me a look which was neither friendly nor unfriendly. *Good* I smiled inwardly.

"Frisk him" he ordered.

Jesus Christ! flashed through my mind. *I am a goner!*

In my right breast pocket I had forgotten my diary full of political anti-Nazi and anti-Soviet statements. (How else could the ideas of a youth be written who had just turned eighteen fighting for his country.) The last page written with righteous anger and threats against the Nazis and the Soviets, in its final words offered "Death to the brown-shirted murderers! Death to the Red traitors who stabbed us in the back!"

My weapons were taken from me and placed on a sofa and all my pockets were emptied.

I watched the commissar while he read the diary page by page. His face seemed to have become friendlier. *But just wait*, I ridiculed myself silently, *until he comes to the last words*. He did and I was observing him carefully, but there were no changes in his facial expression. He eyed me for a short moment, but I detected only curiosity in his look.

Now I will be shot, I thought, *but he will not do it here, if only for the sake of a beautiful Persian carpet, which spattered with blood would lose half of its value. Therefore, he will give the order to shoot me in the courtyard or on the street, and on my way there, perhaps I will have a chance to escape.*

To gain some idea as to what was going to happen to me, I decided to check his friendliness. There was a large box full of fine chocolate-covered cookies on the table.

"Comrade Commissar!" I said casually, "May I take some cookies with me? I haven't had anything to eat the whole day. I am hungry!"

"Take some!"

"Thank you!"

I filled my pockets with the cookies and began eating them right there.

"If you would like it," I mumbled with a mouth full

of cookies, "I could serve in your militia unit. Shall I report to you tomorrow morning?"

"Very well, young man," he answered, "but you have a lot to learn."

"Thank you. I know it!"

"All right," he said turning to the patrol commander. "He may go!"

"Good-night!" I said too quickly, taking my leave.

"Good-night!" he said, and threw my diary into the wastebasket.

Turning around, I surreptitiously observed all the men in the room while walking to the door. Some were sitting at ease on straight chairs and easy chairs, others were standing and conversing in hushed voices.

I closed the door behind me, passing through the hall. The darkness of the staircase enveloped me so suddenly that I had to stop and touch the wall with my hands. My eyes slowly became accustomed to the lack of light and I continued carefully down the stairs.

He didn't give orders to shoot me—I'm sure. I turned it over in my mind. *My age, my truthfulness in the diary, the fact that he threw it away, that he agreed to my service in his unit, and gave me the cookies.* But the last reason felt weak. One gives the condemned man his last wish.

I was still doubting my good luck and looked around carefully after reaching the main gate of the house. A guard stood at the sidewalk opposite the gate. He let me pass without saying a word. I saw him turning his head in my direction when I mounted my horse, waiting for me patiently at the gate.

A CITY IN SURRENDER

I rode into Grodecka Street, but my fortune didn't last long. I was stopped again by a militia patrol. They forbade me to ride further because of the insecure streets. Small arms were still being fired. Two men of the patrol directed me to a nearby stable. I put my horse up and lay down next to him in the corner of his compartment. There were other horses in the stable and some men, but I didn't pay any attention to them. My hand grenades were still in one of my saddlebags. To have a weapon handy, I took one of them out and laid it close to my head. I fell asleep at once thinking about tomorrow.

The Cathedral in Lvov was built in the 13th century as a fortified castle to check Tartar incursions.

LOSING MY HORSE

My sleep left much to be desired. Some peculiar connection between a nightmare and unpleasant reality must have descended upon my world of dreams, for I perceived clearly the voices of men talking in subdued tones in the stable but they were shifting into vivid pictures of the horrors of war. When the first light of the morning finally came through the small windows of the room, I greeted it with relief. My attention turned at once to my horse. Nothing seemed to be wrong with him. He was eating with gusto some fresh hay and grain that I had given him the night before. I opened a tin of canned meat for breakfast, but my appetite failed me. My head was full of turmoil, doubts and uncertainties. The cold water with which I washed myself splashingly brought some freshness. The sight of the hand grenades produced more courage. While packing them my hand almost caressed the cold steel surface of the last efficient weapon still in my possession.

No one in the stable paid any attention to me. Every man there seemed to mind his own business. Without being asked anything by anybody, I rode out into the courtyard which brought me directly into Grodecka Street. Turning west I reflected that there were some one hundred odd kilometers separating me from my family. It was a must that I make them in one piece!

Despite the early hour, male pedestrians crowded the sidewalks. Women evidently did not care yet to venture onto the streets. And who would blame them? All the stores were empty and closed, anyway. The men were mostly young and almost every one wore some pieces of military apparel, indicating that they must have been former soldiers who discarded their uniforms incompletely. Seeing many village faces among them strengthened this opinion. *Away from their homes, just like me,* flashed through my mind.

"Halt!" rang out a shout. "Dismount!"

The commands came from a small man in dark civilian clothing, a cap on his head. My first impression of him was that he decidedly needed some soap and a brush. I had to come to a stop because he held a rifle in his hands pointed toward me. On his left arm he wore a red band. A few passersby stopped and looked at us curiously.

"Whose horse is this?" he asked as he approached.

"It belongs to me. The Polish army requisitioned it during the war. It is the property of my father," I lied without blushing.

"Now there is no private property anymore. Everything is 'kasionniye' (i.e., belonging to the government). Dismount!" he repeated.

"It is impossible for me to do so. I was wounded in the upper left leg" my improvisations continued.

"Hey, you there!" He shouted to some young men gaping at us from the safe distance of the sidewalk. "Help him down!"

Reluctantly, they came over and very carefully,

so as not to hurt my "wound," they lifted me gently from the saddle.

"Set me on the sidewalk," I asked them. They put me on the curb.

The militiaman tried to mount my horse, but because he held a rifle in his left hand, he couldn't do it. Then he hung the rifle on his shoulder. Again he was unable to succeed. My wishes must have been identical with those of the crowd, for many laughed disdainfully. One voice shouted: "Get a cow!" He preferred to overlook the joke and again summoned some young men to his assistance. Only then did he attain the saddle.

He hit the horse with his heels and started to ride back toward the city. The crowd dispersed, for there was nothing more to be seen. I remained sitting at the edge of the sidewalk until the militiaman put five hundred yards between us. Then I got up and began to run slowly after my horse. I got angrier by the minute and decided to recover my four-legged friend in any manner possible, even without knowing at the moment how I would go about it. My purpose grew firmer with every step that brought me closer to the militiaman. Keeping the horse and rider constantly in view, I covered about three miles running and thanking Heaven that in spite of the privations of war my physical condition still permitted me to exert this effort. I was relieved to reach the crowded downtown section of the city because, even if the militiaman turned around now, he would be unable to see me among the multitude of people. Suddenly he turned sharply left into a narrow side street. In less than thirty seconds I was at the turn, but, to my dismay, there was no horse visible. I ran forward quickly and discovered numerous alleys crossing the street. Running its whole length and looking into the side alleys produced no results, so I circled around the entire section of the city many times. In vain. I slowed down and tried to think calmly what to do next. *What, dammit, can be done to get my horse back?* Hundreds and hundreds of thoughts flew through my head like a flock of birds, some black and rapacious, others full of colors and imagination.

As a militiaman, he was armed and thus able to steal my horse. I, too, as a militiaman, would be able to take any counter action to find my horse and to repossess him. This last thought seemed to overwhelm all the previous ones.

The decision was made. Now to implement it. I knocked at random at the very first door of an apartment in the nearest large building. When it opened I asked the woman who appeared for a piece of red cloth out of which an armband could be made. She invited me inside. Ten minutes later the job was done. A bright red shining band was firmly sewn around the sleeve of my clothing. My next step was to report to the headquarters of the militia, located in the prison buildings of Brygitki, and to offer my modest and humble services. After they took down my basic personal data, without asking me for any, absolutely no additional details, I was accepted into this organization. They gave me a rifle and ammunition, a cup of sweetened coffee and dark bread with nothing to smear on it for which I was, nevertheless, grateful. But not too grateful.

LOSING MY HORSE

One of your men has stolen my horse; therefore your just duty is to feed me and keep me until the wrong is righted. When it happens, there will be no difficulty for you in getting rid of me, for I will then go my own way — however, not without certain gratitude, oh mighty militia, which unknowingly helped me to perform a small deed of simple human justice.

My first assignment consisted of receiving, at a large table, all arms and military objects or equipment which the population was ordered to surrender. It was some job! Old, scared men and women were attempting to show their loyalty to the new owners of the city, and they were bringing everything, from military buttons with the Polish eagle imprinted on them, to green handkerchiefs of army issue. It was one of the few times in my life that I almost lost faith in the Polish people as a nation of patriots. One old man brought with him a superb hunting knife whose large handle, incrusted with mother-of-pearl in a highly artistic fashion, shone beautifully in the sun. He asked whether this knife had to be considered a weapon. The militiaman sitting next to me answered quickly:

"Of course, naturally, what else do you think?" He took it from the hands of the old fellow. But I became curious as to his honesty.

Is he going to deliver this piece of decoration to the storage room where we are taking all the items we collect, or will he take it for himself?

While working at his side and with my eyes only, encouraging all the people who came to our table, my attention was concentrated on this knife. When the time came to load the arms into large sacks and take them to storage, I made sure that it was I who stood up and started to load them. I picked up a pile of army bayonets together with the shining knife. My companion moved suddenly to my side.

"I will help you!" he said.

"Thanks! It is not heavy," was my answer. "I can manage it all alone."

"Oh, no! Let's go!"

He helped me to carry it. When we arrived in the storage room and shook out the arms, he took the hunting knife, put it under his loose jacket, and secured it to his body with a piece of string which he wound around himself above the waist.

"If you find something you like," he said without looking at me, "make sure you take it. If *you* don't someone else will, so, what's the difference?"

"Thank you. I will," I lied, knowing full well that he would not make a common thief out of me.

Our shift came to an end soon and we were relieved by other militiamen. I was spending all my free time in the huge stables in which horses of the former Polish army were kept and where I searched for the only horse I wanted, my own. It would have been easy for me to take any of the tens of thousands of horses, some of which were more beautiful and energetic than mine, but that was not my purpose. I searched and searched. I knew that the thief could not have kept my horse for himself, but must have delivered him to one of the stables. As it turned out, I was wrong. I learned that it was possible to own a horse for business reasons, for instance, transportation. So I contacted all known transportation houses and went through their livestock—all in vain.

One evening I almost thought that I had found him, but it was only a striking similarity that deceived me at a distance. Coming closer I saw that it was not he.

One of my uncles bumped into me accidentally on the street one day. He was appalled at the sight of my red armband. I explained the situation, but found no understanding in his eyes.

"Don't you know what's going on?" he asked me. "They have arrested all officers whom they found at home, all judges, court personnel, policemen, community leaders, political figures, even some N.C.O.'s. Quite a few landowners, even the small ones, were thrown out of their homes, some shot summarily without due process of law. They practically do not feed their prisoners everybody in their prisons is starving—no medical attention there, either. . .!"

"Yes," was my answer, "many people told me about it—also the men at the militia headquarters. What can be done about it?"

He looked at me coolly and said "Good-bye."

Dismayed by the generally bad situation as well as the negative results of the search for my horse, I nevertheless continued looking for him. It seemed to me that I had covered all the large and the small stables, but there was still hope that I would find the only horse I cared for and the only one I wanted. I slept little and tried to work as little as possible at the arms collecting unit, thus leaving more time to spend on searching. All seemed to lead to nothing.

In the meantime many people questioned me in reference to the future. As a militiaman, I was expected to know. Actually, a simple employee of the—as we thought then—"regular" police force, i.e., militia, was kept in the dark in all matters of not only higher politics, but also of lower echelon political activities. He only knew whom to arrest after being told the names of the unfortunate ones. But even for the militia and its higher organs, i.e., the Soviet political police, it was difficult to operate in a city whose population swelled from two hundred and fifty thousand before the war to nearly half a million. The influx included all the military men who flocked to Lvov, the unshakable bastion of defense, as well as the refugees. The lot of the refugees was not enviable. They had to live wherever they found a bit of shelter—in churches, convents, monasteries, huts, and in conditions comparable to an inferno. Their food supplies exhausted, they had to beg or to exchange all their valuables for food. Inconceivably rapacious human hyenas took advantage of their deplorable situation. I stole food from the canteen of the militia and distributed it at random to the children I met. They would take it and quickly run home with it. I saw people shot in revenge to "even up the score" for wrongs, real or imagined, dating from before the war.

On a hot morning, the third day of my work as a militiaman, I stood in the shaded entrance of a building, taking refuge from the already oppressive heat despite the early hour, when a man entered the hall.

"Gene!" I shouted. It was an old soccer team buddy from my home town. We had played on opposite teams, but liked and respected each other.

"What are you doing here?. . .and with this!" he pointed at my red armband.

I gave a rapid account of my activities. He shook his head in amazement while I tried to be as matter-of-fact and cool as possible in my narration. He listened and finally concluded:

"It is no time to regret the roses, when the forests are burning! Let's go home!"

I pondered for a long moment as he waited patiently. I took off the red armband, put my rifle in the far corner of the hall and while he smiled, I said:

"Let's go! What are we waiting for?"

The late Renaissance Boimov Chapel, erected 1609-1617 by the wealthy burghers of Lvov.

GOING HOME — THE FIRST DAY

The day had become very sultry, but we knew that we had to leave Lvov at once if we were to reach Przemysl on foot in two or three days. We knew that we had to pass through country touched by war. There would be difficulties in procuring food. The shooting was not yet over, because the advancing Soviet army was encountering resistance from well-organized Polish military units which were attempting to cross over into Rumania or Hungary. We didn't know how far toward the West the Germans were withdrawing, but we were quite sure that we could overcome any obstacle they might place for us.

Gene was carrying a light canvas shoulder bag with food and another smaller handbag with his private belongings. I relieved him by taking the latter, and from then on our steps quickened. We reached the western outskirts of the city without incident. We understood then why the German army was unable to enter Lvov from this direction. An ingenious system of defense had been constructed, with connecting deep ditches running in all directions, with high anti-tank barricades made of heavy trunks of felled trees and various other impediments—all placed in positions perfectly suited to the natural features of the terrain. Everywhere there was destruction caused by heavy artillery and aerial bombing.

Many houses, both large and small, and suburban farms had been burned or destroyed either totally or partially by the shelling.

In the first hour of our march we made four miles, which was rather comforting, but we realized that we were walking too fast if we wanted to keep on until dusk, so we slowed down. We were constantly passing two human waves, one moving in the opposite direction from ours, the other, much slower, went west with us. We spoke to many people as we passed them without stopping. We wanted to know how far from us were the Soviet spearhead units, as well as the bulk of their forces. That information was vital. We knew that we could not pass through their marching formations and that it would be necessary to work around them.

And indeed, after we had covered another five miles we were told by a highway militiaman who barred our way, that we could not proceed further, because there was fighting going on directly ahead. We had heard some shots a few minutes before, but we had assumed that some young village boys were having fun with rifles found in the fields, an occurrence which had become common. We turned back a few hundred yards to be out of sight of the militiaman, then cut straight to the north. In about half an hour we reached a railroad line which ran east-west. Continuing west along the iron tracks, we knew full well that it must lead us to Przemysl.

During a short rest stop we relaxed and ate what we had. Gene gave me some bread which I ate heartily with apples picked near the road. For dessert I had slices of sugar beets. They were abundant in the fields through which we passed and naturally I had picked some. It was with some reluctance that we got on our feet again. Sitting on the soft grass was very relaxing and we procrastinated for a few minutes in the cool shade of the tree.

Continuing our march, we noted that the heat of the day was gone and a fresh breeze helped us walk faster, but the evening was close at hand, so we had to seek shelter. Two hours later we came to the large village of Suchowola. We decided to spend the night there, but of course we didn't have any idea how or where. After a short consultation, I went into the village looking for the mayor, but unexpectedly I was informed by two women, whom I asked about the whereabouts of the mayor's house, that there was an empty schoolhouse in which we could sleep. They seemed to understand my need for shelter without being told, and they were so polite that they even walked with me to the school and entered the building with me. What a sight! The whole floor was covered with scattered books, many savagely torn apart. Innumerable loose pages littered the premises. A few volumes remained on the wooden shelves of glass covered cases, but there was very little glass left in them. Destructive hands had broken it into thousands of fragments and it lay all around, glittering in the red rays of the evening sun. Without a word I began to pick up the books from the floor and to place them on the shelves. The two women stood idly for a moment and then assisted me, and the room was cleaned up in a few minutes. I went out to bring in Gene, who had waited patiently for me at the spot in the grove where I had left him.

As we entered the school several new people had arrived to spend the night, and were busying themselves with the necessary preparations. I went exploring in other rooms, which were also occupied by refugees of various ages, some with children, others with heavy luggage, many in rags and all tired. They spoke animatedly, asking each other innumerable questions to which there were no easy answers. Nobody knew what the immediate future would bring.

In a large wall credenza I found two large empty burlap sacks. I put one into another, thus making it twice as strong, connected the two bottom corners by two pieces of heavy cord with the top, making a tough knapsack. I started to fill it with books I liked, but darkness interrupted me and I had to return to my corner where Gene was already asleep, snoring loudly. I lay down near him, but no matter how welcome the pine floor felt to the touch of my fingers, it was too hard for me to rest on it comfortably. I took books from the improvised knapsack and spread them evenly under me. Then I was able to achieve a degree of comfort.

Thinking about the miles separating me from home made me more tired. One thought in particular bothered me and kept coming back to mind: *Is everything all right with the family? Is our house still standing? Maybe it was bombed?* There was nothing I could do in either case, and I attempted to abandon negative thoughts of matters over which I had no control. All my energy had to be directed toward reaching my home town by the shortest possible route, and we had not yet crossed the lines of the advancing Soviet army, which presented an immediate goal.

The peaceful breathing of tired men, women and children, who were all asleep, made me drowsy, and my eyelids became heavier; I did not even notice when I fell asleep. My last semi-conscious awareness was of some distant shots which I seemed to hear, but I didn't know whether they were a part of my dreams or not. . .

GOING HOME – THE SECOND DAY

The sun shining through the window under which we were sleeping awakened me, and for a moment I didn't know where I was. Slowly turning my head I perceived the walls lined with bookshelves, then Gene and other people, all still asleep. I remembered the previous evening with all its details. The regular breathing of my companions and their deep slumber in spite of the daylight proved their extreme fatigue, but I didn't feel tired at all. Silently I thanked my teachers for instilling in us the necessity of strenuous physical exercise.

Was it time to get up? Quietly, I went outdoors, washed, and walked to the village looking for breakfast. I found it at a house full of children, whose parents refused to accept any money from me. Returning to the schoolhouse I awakened Gene. He seemed not to want to get up, but after further urging he did, for he too understood that time was of the essence. The coffee with which I had filled my canteen strengthened him somewhat. A few minutes later we hit the road west, but not before filling my knapsack with books which I chose carefully for future leisure.

To walk the railroad line we had to shorten our steps to adjust them to the spacing of the ties. I smiled to myself observing the rhythm to which we had to adjust ourselves. It was like some kind of crazy ballet: six or seven short steps, two long ones and again six or

152

seven short, etc. It became a very tiring sequence, so from time to time we stepped away from the well-beaten path, but found soon that the going through the grass was still rougher. We returned again to the railroad ties.

Around noon we reached the city of Grodek and, oh, wonder, there was a steaming locomotive ready to roll! The machinist was a young boy, who had learned to operate it. He accepted us as passengers after a bit of financial encouragement. Standing at the large window near the engine we enjoyed each kilometer that we were passing, sometimes fast, sometimes slowly when the rails were weakened by bombing and only partially repaired. To our dismay we had to abandon this speedy "iron horse." The railroad line near Sadova Vishnia showed total destruction. Only the engineer appeared unmoved, probably because he saw some passengers who wanted to travel back in the direction from which we came. We paid, thanked him and continued on foot.

The air became sultry and the heat got worse. We walked slowly, saving our energy for later.

On the western outskirts of the city we were stopped by a Soviet military unit. They were prohibiting any movement to the west without offering the slightest explanation. We turned around but as soon as we were out of sight of the soldiers we circled north around them looking for a rugged, wooded terrain that would provide us with shelter and cover from the Soviet patrols. There were shots in the distance at irregular intervals. Mostly machine gun and rifle fire and only seldom a louder explosion of hand grenades. We moved carefully, trying to avoid making noise. An hour later we reached the tracks again which we had left earlier. We quickened the march until it was certain that we must have passed the advancing Red Army and that we were in no-man's-land.

It was dark when we entered a village near the railroad. Our first impressions were of unusual traffic within the locality. *The Germans are here—*I thought. A farmer whom I asked about them confirmed my guess. We could go back again and circle around the Germans, but we came here to find a safe place for Gene, who was near physical collapse and needed some peace and quiet. I found a farmer's family who agreed to let him lie down in bed until I went to Przemysl and brought somebody from his family with means for transporting him. Before leaving I checked his pulse: it was darn fast. The measurement of his temperature revealed that it was much too high for comfort. I cursed under my breath while outwardly showing him a smiling unconcerned face and joking about his light flu, but I knew that he had to have medical attention as soon as possible. I told the host that if no one came to fetch him within the next twenty-four hours he should be transported to the nearest hospital some five miles distant from the village. I would return for Gene myself, should his family be unable to take him. The farmer, a friendly middle-aged man, promised me solemnly to do as he was told. I left quickly.

Outside I heard the idling motors of cars. Upon coming closer I saw German soldiers being loaded into trucks hurriedly by an officer. I decided to try my luck and asked him whether he would be going to Przemysl. He looked at me searchingly, but my German language must have made a good impression on him. He not only answered affirmatively, but also asked whether it was my destination also. After a short conversation he gave me permission to mount one of his trucks. I did it instantly. Inside the truck hung a small kerosene lamp and in its weak light I discerned some figures sitting on the side benches: German soldiers and Polish railroaders in their uniforms. The Poles didn't talk, but the Germans were vocal and conversed loudly and animatedly about going home. I smiled to myself. I knew that they would be retained by the army. *England and France must be fighting you*—I thought—*and you may as well forget about your homes.* Questioning the railroaders I learned that the Ruskis would occupy Poland up to the San-Bug line and their German friends the territories west of it. I sighed and became silent.

The trucks were moving fast. Within half an hour we covered about 30 kilometers and arrived in Przemysl. My joy was great, but it ended at the very moment the trucks stopped: they brought us into the prisoner-of-war camp.

Hm, I thought, *how in the heck can I get out of here?*

The lieutenant who brought us here was reporting at attention to a major. I approached quickly and politely greeted them.

"Sir"—I addressed the major—"This gentleman"—I pointed to the lieutenant—"brought me here, but I am not a prisoner-of-war. I asked him for transportation to Przemysl and he obliged me. My family lives here—not too far from this place. I was not in the Polish Armed

Forces for I am still too young," I lied with a straight face while looking directly in his eyes.

In Prussian dialect he barked a question to the lieutenant. Standing at attention he confirmed my coming to his unit.

"All right," said the major. "Go home."

I bowed my head both to thank him and to say "Good-bye".

I preferred not to salute him either in the military or in the Nazi manner. Leaving the officers I kept the lieutenant in sight, waiting for him to be alone. Indeed, after a few minutes' conversation with his superior he walked away toward a barrack building. I followed quickly.

"Sir," I approached him, "could you be so kind as to notify the guard at the gate that a free passage was given to me. I would be very obliged for your kindness."

Without a word, as if performing an unpleasant duty, he strode with importance to the large gate and informed the appropriate sergeant about my permission to leave the compound, adding that I was to wait for the next batch of prisoners-of-war to be transported out of the camp and that I had to walk with the guards, for the curfew hours were imposed upon the city and at this hour a civilian wandering through the streets would be shot on sight. Listening carefully to him I tried to determine his accent. It was unclear to me whether it was Bavarian or Austrian.

Hm—I thought,—*this fellow is not a bad one. Let me show him my gratitude for his giving me free transportation, for backing me up in front of the major and for*

GOING HOME · THE SECOND DAY

his accomodating my latter request! I thanked him in
nice, polite expressions and extended a twenty zlotys
note to him saying that it was the least I could do for
him. He smiled, thanked me, said good-bye, saluted the
N.C.O. while simultaneously turning his face toward me
and left. Placing myself close to the gate I directed all
my senses to observing the constant movement of men
around me. The Germans were the first of my priorities.
They were all young, both the soldiers on guard duty and
the others coming and going through the gate in small
formations. Every soldier or officer wore a camouflage
jacket, some even whole suits. Their movements were
precise and uniform, thus in a marching formation all
heads faced only one direction—forward, none of their
helmets swerved either right or left. Their steps reminded
me of highly trained ballet dancers minus the grace for
which my eyes searched in vain. After some moments I
was able to perceive subconsciously a certain heaviness
with which their limbs seemed to be endowed like the
heavy mechanism of large church clocks that strike the
hour with overwhelming irreversible force. Their rigid
bodies looked as if they were unable to bend without difficulty, so straight, erect and stiff. *Automats*—I thought—
*but thinking automats, who followed every order of their
leaders with utmost efficiency, without the slightest
doubt and hesitation. On the contrary, with great drive,
deep personal pride and an egotistical attitude which gave
the impression that each of them wanted to be more perfect than the next man in the row.* Without realizing it
a sigh escaped my lips. I became aware of it only when I
caught myself holding my breath.

My attention turned to the Polish prisoners-of-war, who seemed to be everywhere. Swarms of them walked slowly and haltingly, as if stumbling over some small invisible obstacles. Many wore bandages around their heads or arms, hands in slings, whose original white had become a grey, others helping themselves with canes or just simple sticks—all wearing bloody or soil-stained uniforms or their remnants, many bareheaded, unkempt, unshaved and filthy. They talked to each other, but their heads hung low and hunger marked their haggard faces. Others sat huddling close together, covering themselves with their military great coats. I shuddered on this hot, sultry night. With my head bathed in sweat I suddenly became cold and shivered again.

"Form the column!" The German shout brought me back to reality. German soldiers were efficient. In less than two minutes their prisoners were standing in a neat marching formation, three soldiers in each row. The gate was thrown open and flanked on both sides by the German armed guards the Poles marched out. I came closer to the N.C.O. at the gate and reminded him to tell a passing guard that I was not a prisoner, which he did promptly and I made sure to keep at the side of the guard to whom I talked from time to time about insignificant trifles. Within fifteen minutes we reached the downtown section of the city and I took leave from the guard, who in a friendly manner warned me not to get shot so near to home. My fears about any danger while alone on the road were over. Nothing could happen to me now at the place where each house was long familiar and every un-

GOING HOME - THE SECOND DAY

even spot in the surface of the sidewalk was not strange either.

Not one living soul was on the streets. I walked fast, but carefully, and my heavy army boots didn't seem to make any noise on the stones. Fifty yards up Franciscan Street, sharp left turn into Vladich, up the steep hill along the ancient walls of the fortress, another left and forty yards before making a sharp right and continuing along my own street up the hill.

*Will the house be standing or. . .*I didn't dare to finish my thought, but kept walking fast in darkness until I reached our garden on the left. Slowing down, I strained my eyes and approaching slowly I made out the dark contours of the building. Entering the front veranda I stood still and listened. *Thank Heaven!* Through the window I heard voices inside. Coming closer to the window I recognized the voices of my mother and my brother. My gentle knock at the window caused instant stillness in the apartment. I could hear my heart beat. I knocked again somewhat harder.

"Robert!" exclaimed mother, recognizing my manner of knocking. A heavy curtain parted slightly to the side, and light from the kitchen fell on our faces. "Oh!"— she shouted again and I heard her steps through the kitchen, through the hall and a second later the door opened. Without a word she embraced me and like every mother in a similar situation she started to sob.

"Get him in!" urged Marion. She let go of me and I stepped in. As we shook hands my brother and I looked long into each other's eyes...

It was good to be home!. . .

A DAY WITH THE GERMANS

The warmth and the light of day awakened me gently and gradually. It felt late, and a quick glance at my watch showed noon. Looking around me, I perceived no changes in the good old bedroom since I left it three weeks ago. Everything was as before the war. Mother tiptoed in after a while and, seeing me awake, backed up through the door, only to reappear in a brief moment with breakfast on a tray. She asked uncounted questions and had to content herself with my nods yes or no. I concentrated on the food, wolfing it down. Fortunately, my brother appeared in the door and interrupted the incessant flow of Mother's words. Thanking him with a smile, I continued eating with gusto until the plate was empty. When I asked for seconds, Mother brought more instantly. Now, I was the one who threw questions at them.

"Are the Germans still in the city?"

"Yes. But they are leaving."

"For where?"

"For the western bank of the San River. The Bolsheviks are to come in. The San will be the border line between them."

"Impossible!"

"Now, everything is possible!"

"You mean to tell me that the city will be cut in half?"

"That's just about the story."

A DAY WITH THE GERMANS

We fell silent thinking about it. Przemysl, this ancient city of Poland with origins reaching back to the fifth century or even earlier, one of the strongest fortresses of the Commonwealth and its southeastern bastion, had never been divided. Now that I think of it, there was one exception. For a few hours on November 1, 1918, the Ukrainians, supplied by the Austrians with arms and ammunition, surprised the Poles in the wee hours of the early morning and occupied the eastern bank of the San together with the heart of the city. They seemed not to have cared for the left bank city. There the Poles organized and launched such a strong attack that within a few hours the city was freed and reunited.

"Let me get dressed," I said. "I have things to do before the frontier is established and firmly guarded."

"Going away again?" asked Mother in a tone of disapproval and reproach.

"Only to return!"

She left the room and I started to dress. In a few minutes I left the house wearing a dark sport suit and hurried downtown to see what the situation was. The streets were full of people in a hurry. A sour smell of a conflagration hit my nostrils when I reached Yagiellon Street, and I saw a building in flames: the synagogue. It was one of the oldest, important monumental landmarks of the city. The presence of the Jewish community in Przemysl can be traced to the year 1002 A.D. Now it was burning! In front of it, on the sidewalk across the broad street, stood a group of a few dozen German soldiers and officers, many of whom photographed the fire raging in and outside the place of worship and the dense clouds of smoke pouring out of this condemned-by-man house of God.

Only my urgent assignment in the suburb of Zasanie on the western bank of the river prevented me from stopping and looking around; I decided to do it later, for now I had to notify the family of Gene about his illness and inability to reach home. He had fallen sick in a village about twenty kilometers east of the city and awaited his relatives to come and fetch him. Now I hurried to their home to inform them promptly of his situation and whereabouts. Two of his brothers went immediately to arrange transportation. They did it so quickly that I was quite surprised by their fast return while I was still talking with their mother. They found an old Ford jalopy with an exceptionally loud-running motor, but it ran and that was the main thing. The young men knew very well that if the German-Russian border should be established along the San River they would be cut off from their brother Gene who lay ill east of the town. They decided to hurry to him, and I was all for it. They asked me if they could offer me a ride back home and I accepted, for it did not take them out of their way. We got in and we talked while riding.

"Do you need my help with Gene? Should I direct you to him? Will it not be easier for you if I go with you?" I asked them.

"Thank you—thanks again, but you have done enough already and we are in your debt. We are familiar with the village he is in and it will not be difficult at all for us to take care of him. Please, direct us to your home."

A DAY WITH THE GERMANS

"I am not going home. Any spot near the center of the city will do perfectly," I answered, and did not insist on accompanying them. The car was small and there was not enough room for three persons in the front. The fourth would have to lay on the backseat to minimize the discomfort of travel while being sick.

"Stop here any place," I said as we reached the narrow winding streets of the old section of the city.

They thanked me again. One of them graciously opened the car door for me and shook my hand in gratitude and asked me to turn to them for assistance if ever I should need any. Slightly embarrassed, I waved to them and watched their car until it disappeared around the nearby bend.

Heading for the burning synagogue by the shortest way, I walked through the old alleys of the Jewish section, where there was always traffic, noise, and movement. Now there was not a single passerby, and an uncanny stillness reigned all around. It felt, however, as if invisible eyes were observing me from the windows of the numerous apartment buildings I was passing. It was understandable that the Jews locked themselves in their rooms as soon as the Germans occupied Przemysl and did not dare to go out into the open for fear of their lives. I recalled my brother's information this noon about the execution by shooting of some prominent Jewish merchants by the Germans as soon as they entered the city. Those well-known members of the commercial Jewish community, now dead, were boycotting merchandise imported from Germany. Their display windows announced with large signs—"We do not sell German products." This was their crime in the eyes of their Nazi executioners.

The Jewish minority in Poland was very well informed about the situation of their brethren in Germany and was instrumental, from 1935 on, in bringing over half a million Jews out of Germany and German-annexed Austria, Bohemia, Moravia and Slovakia. The latter had been made independent by Hitler, but they were not too safe for the Jews. There was a long tradition of cooperation and friendship between the Jews and the Poles. As a popular saying expressed it, "every Pole has his own Jew," which simply meant that each Pole was to a degree dependent on a certain Jew no matter whether "his" Jew was his doctor, lawyer, pharmacist, butcher, shoemaker, ice cream man, book store owner or clerk.

So-called Polish anti-Semitism was a bad, unreal, Kafkaish nightmare invented by the Nazi press, to whom even the Western correspondents and their public listened attentively. The Germans tried to excuse their own historical anti-Jewish feelings which permeated the centuries from the medieval ages to the little eighteenth-century Rothschild money-lending shop in Frankfurt. The very presence of three and a half million Jews in Poland before the outbreak of the Second World War is the best refutation of the unfounded insinuations and falsehoods expounded by the Western press before 1939. It was the Nazis, the most unlikely agents, who were able to discredit the Poles in the eyes of the West as an anti-Semitic nation. However, the truth is that the Jews were far too intelligent to have lived for centuries in a country in which there was discrimination against them. Had discrimination existed in Poland they would have left it as they left Spain, Italy, the Netherlands, Belgium, England, Germany, Austria, etc., where only small numbers remained. Poland, on the contrary, was considered by them a "second" and sometimes a "first" promised land, for they felt well and secure there. *"Oh Poland, oh kingly land, in which we have lived happily for many centuries. . ."* begins one of the religious cantos of Polish Jews. Moses Isserless, a Jewish rabbi and a very learned scholar in Talmud, wrote to one of his disciples who had returned from Germany to Poland:"I am glad to hear you have returned in good health . . . It is better to eat dry bread in our country (Poland), where the hatred is not so great as in Germany. May it remain so until the coming of the Messiah. . ."

All these thoughts crossed my mind as I walked to another pogrom committed by the Nazis on Polish soil, in my hometown—this time the victim was a synagogue. I approached the building from the rear and rejoiced at the fact that it was not damaged by fire from this direction. There was a sudden movement and a slight noise in front of me. Stepping through the door, I saw a young boy, maybe eighteen, dressed in Hasidic attire, carrying a box on his shoulders. On seeing me, he stopped and looked at me with uncertainty in his dark eyes, but I quieted him quickly, speaking to him. A short conversation ensued and a few moments later we were both carrying valuables out of the burning premises and depositing them in nearby houses for further disposal. Stumbling over the rubble on the floor, hot from the fire that raged in the north side of the building, choking and blinded by the low-hanging smoke, we carried on our work for which there was no reward. The boy told me that there were dynamite charges laid under the synagogue by the Germans, but I discounted this possibility. There were too many large apartment houses in the immediate proximity and the street adjacent to the north of the building was used by the Germans as one of their main communication arteries. It had to be kept open for their own convenience. A few more boys, both Polish and Jewish, who must have observed us without being seen, lent us helping hands. Soon we had done our work. There was nothing more of any value left inside. We dispersed without saying much, each of us going his own way, but surely feeling better. . .

My next self-imposed assignment involved a social visit. At a time when people were still being killed and houses burned and destroyed? Oh, yes! Because it involved my friend Stefanie! Blond and pretty, she was a little neurotic, with some assumed airs in her behavior; proud but sweet, she visibly preferred me over all the other boys. She had associated with many at school dances, sporting events, concerts, theatres, and other social events. But she went to the movies only with me or with her older sister. Spoiled in a nice way by her three older sisters and one brother, she was a beautiful girl. Her whole family approved of our rather platonic friendship, which lasted over four years. There were my visits at her home, or hers at mine, when even my mother seemed not to mind it too much and showed interest only by not leaving us alone for too long a time when there was no one else around. To our misfortune, there was almost always some one in our way—my brother, my aunt or uncle or grandfather or just one of my numerous friends who seemed to be coming to our home so often that Mother jokingly called our apartment "the railroad station."

I liked Stefanie very much. She liked me too and became one of my very special pals in the years of our acquaintance. My visit at her home today was at least appropriate, if not necessary. The problem was that she lived in Zasanie and nobody knew when a firm border would be established along the river. It could happen at any moment. If it happened while I was visiting her, I would be cut off from my home and family. I had to find out about it first, simply not to get shot during the first day at home.

I circled around the synagogue and came out at the same place in front of the building where I had been earlier. The broad thoroughfare was active with general movement toward the west. The heavy German military traffic was evident even to an untrained eye. Some formations marched, while other units rode in canvas covered army trucks. Numerous soldiers were walking at ease, as if on furlough, and quite a few of them stopped before the burning synagogue talking, smiling and photographing it. Observing them carefully, but maintaining an outwardly casual expression, I noticed that not all smiled. I crossed the street and started a conversation with two of them. At first they eyed me with distrust, but in the course of small talk they relaxed and we exchanged polite pleasantries. I complimented them on their fine

victory, their organization, and asked them very inno-
cently how long they would remain in my hometown.
They replied that they had to be on the other side of the
river at dusk, for the Russians would come here tonight.

"Will you not come with us to the western
bank?"—one of them suddenly asked. For a split second I
lost my composure, not expecting such an invitation, but
I recovered instantly.

"Well," I answered slowly, "it would be a good
idea. The only difficulty is that my mother, brother and
the whole family lives here. We have a house here and it
would not be easy for us to come right away. But if we
do not like the Russians, we certainly will try to reach our
distant relatives in Krakow."

They smiled and a short silence ensued among us.
I knew what I wanted to know, but I also realized that
there was not much time between now and dusk. Re-
maining and talking for another few moments for the
sake of appearances, was a social and tactical must. Only
after the elapse of appropriate time did I take my leave
politely and walked slowly away. Out of their sight I resumed the brisk walk of someone on an errand, crossed
the temporary wooden bridge on the river. A few minutes
later I knocked at the door of Stefanie's parents.

"Who is there?" asked a feminine voice through the
door.

"Robert. Is Stefanie at home?"

"Yes, yes. Come in. Come in."

It was Stefanie's sister who let me in and led me to
the living room. Four women were working on Polish

army uniforms, changing them into civilian attire. I greeted them and they expessed genuine joy at seeing me, for no information about me had been available from any source. After the flow of words by her mother and sisters finally ceased, Stefanie moved closer.

"Many times I have asked your mother about you, but she did not know anything and did not receive any news about you. It is good to see you. How are you? What are your plans? Do you know that we will be separated by the border? How long can you stay?" She was blushing sweetly while asking the questions.

With the best smile I could muster, I answered her.

"I don't know. Nobody knows. Hm, how long can I stay? Perhaps for a half an hour . . . until the dusk falls. I only wanted to be sure that nothing happened to you,—that you were well,—and your family too. I'm happy that everything is all right with you . . ."

We crossed over to a little parlor where we were alone. Her father and brother Emil were away from home collecting military uniforms from Polish soldiers who had hidden from the Germans. They had to have civilian-looking outfits in order to be able to reach their homes without being apprehended as former soldiers. I wondered about the family's actions. Being Ukrainian, their mercy mission towards the Poles was open to question. Two explanations were possible—first, that they helped only their Ukrainian brothers which was not so much unthinkable as unnecessary, because Ukrainians in Polish uniforms caught by the Germans were released to go home; second, that in spite of their Ukrainian nationality they were loyal Polish citizens performing their human duties and assisting those who needed help. The latter possibility seemed to be more plausible than the former, because in Stefanie's family there could not have been any enmity against the Poles. Stefanie's older sister, Sophie, was married to a Polish officer; Lucy, another sister, gravitated toward the Polish educational system, being a teacher; Maria, the oldest of the girls, was active in Polish socio-political organizations; their father, a retired Polish government employee, preferred the Polish suitors of his daughters to their Ukrainian competitors. The personality of young Emil was rather quiet, and he certainly did not belong to any Ukrainian chauvinist group that had worked with the Germans before the war to overthrow the Polish government by force.

Stefanie and I spoke in low tones about the great unknown, the future toward which Stefanie was looking without despair. Quite the contrary, she displayed an attitude of belief and faith in herself, her family and friends. Sitting together we forgot about the war and its privations and hardships. We would certainly have continued as in the pre-war times, for we were young, alive, and ready to love, but it must have been the devil, or perhaps an angel, who made me look at my watch. It was almost seven o'clock. Another look through the window confirmed the late hour. It was getting dark.

"You cannot go home now. It is dangerous," remonstrated Stefanie. "You know that the Germans are looking to pick up more prisoners of war. In the evening they carefully check the papers of anyone who is on the street even *before* the curfew. Stay with us tonight, Robert. There is enough room for you."

A DAY WITH THE GERMANS

"Sorry," was my answer. "You realize that my duty lies back home and that the border will be put up firmly at any moment. Maybe it has already happened. Listen, let fate decide. If I cannot get through tonight, I shall return at once without trying again in the darkness, but if I can, well . . . I will visit you anyhow. In any case do not worry. Let's see what destiny has in store for us tonight."

She agreed reluctantly and sadly smiled one of her pretty smiles while kissing me "good-bye." I took leave of her mother and sisters, who also wanted to detain me, but this time permitted me to have my way.

Leaving their home I planned my route, choosing not the shortest way, but the least frequented one, through the short side streets, alleys, and narrow passages. All went well until I reached the wooden bridge on the river. A German guard stopped me saying that the bridge was being taken apart and passage was impossible. Indeed, at the opposite side of the bridge I saw dozens of soldiers carrying heavy beams, boards and planks toward us. The pieces of lumber were parts of the bridge. My heart sank, but I told the guard in my most exquisite German that I had to see the commanding officer of this engineering unit at once. I was certain he must be present supervising the work. The guard let me pass. I stepped on the surface of the bridge and I reached its end unhindered. Yes, the guard was right—about ten yards of boards had been removed. I reported to the officer in charge who said flatly "no" to my request and smilingly pointed with his hand to the space empty of planks. The rippling dark water of the quickly flowing river appeared to laugh at me.

"You see yourself," he said, "it is impossible."

"It is possible. I will jump it."

"It is dangerous. You will not make it."

"I will make it easily. Let me take a look."

Our short conversation attracted a number of eavesdropping soldiers.

"Let him jump, lieutenant, sir!" exclaimed a smiling sergeant to a roar of laughing approval from the group. Other soldiers, busy until now, stopped their work as if on command. Calmly, I took a deep breath, came closer to the broad abyss and examined it. My first impression was correct. *I can make it, indeed,* I thought, *but only because there is a difference in the jump levels in my favor.* The level of the bridge was about two yards higher than the soft shore upon which I had to land after the jump. Otherwise the jump could not be made. The soldiers became quiet, taking a sympathetic interest in my contest and plight. I felt they were for me and for my success and that they considered the whole incident from a challenging sportive point of view.

"Could you direct your lights to the edge?" I turned to the lieutenant. Even before his commanding voice reached the soldiers at two strong reflectors, they had begun to turn them to the desired direction.

I was ready. I took another good look from the edge to the shore and asked the onlookers to make some room for my forerun to jump. They parted to both sides of the narrow bridge, thus making a kind of a long corridor: It was my runway. I was lightly dressed and my sport shoes were excellent for the purpose, because their rubber soles and heels lent themselves perfectly to jumping. In order to be entirely on the safe side I removed my jacket and tie and handed them to a soldier standing near me with a request to throw them over to me afterwards. He smiled and nodded agreement.

God help me. In the name of the Father... I crossed myself mentally and started to run as fast as I could. Still more speed...here comes the edge...bounce high... and I flew through the air over the black water...the water began to close up with the speed of lightning...I had a momentary flash that I would not make it...and I landed! My left foot was in the mud of the shore, the right on the firm ground. I fell lightly on the grass.

"Hurrah! Hurrah!" rang the acknowledging shouts of the German soldiers at the bridge who clapped their hands loudly. I felt like an actor after a successful performance and waved back to them. My jacket came flying past me and wrapped in it I found a piece of hard wood to facilitate the throw. I raised my hand again in a gesture of thanks, picked up the jacket and retrieved my left shoe that had gotten stuck in the soft mud of the river edge. Then still using the dark side streets I rushed home and slept the sleep of the just.

MAUSER 98

Born in the city of Radom in 1938 in the factory at the State Armaments Works, her last name was Mauser 98 and at baptism, instead of a Christian first name she was given the number 169921.

She was a worthy representative of the Polish army issue rifles, used as infantry weapons during the September, 1939 campaign. All her metallic outer parts, oxidized black, lent an impression of seriousness and dignity. Like an elegant woman wearing a black gown, she was dolled up for the ballroom of the war, where death was leading the dance. Her brown wooden parts reminded one of the healthy mahogany tan of the young Greek goddesses and her shape was similar to that of a beautiful magic scepter of a good godmother from a fairy tale. She descended from a high aristocratic family, because in the coat of arms engraved on her steel barrel she had a crowned eagle.

Her original owner was a simple private, a small farmer's son with a Byelo-Russian name, who drove a grain cart and was attached to the supply train of the squadron of the divisional cavalry of the 38th Division of the Reserve Infantry commanded by Colonel Wir-Konas (he perished later in the infamous Katyn woods). As he led the horses, the soldier alternately put his rifle to one side then the other of his body, as if she were impeding him. After I had noticed it I turned to him:

"Would you allow, sir, that I take care of your rifle?"

"Yes," he muttered under his breath with no great enthusiasm. But I noticed that a faint smile of satisfaction appeared on his face, probably because I addressed him as "sir."

"But in case of need, please return her to me."

"Good. Thank you."

I took care of this most valuable new acquisition of mine according to an old N.C.O.'s admonition to the recruits: "The rifle must be cherished and loved as if she were your own fiancee, for she must function perfectly if needed."

Ten days later there were enough rifles for everybody. They were not lying on the ground as yet, but I saw that some soldiers were already carrying two of them, and therefore I reasoned that the former owner of my rifle could not make any pretensions to me like "Give me back my rifle," the more so because in the meanwhile I received, to have at my disposal, a brand new motorcycle, a "Falcon 1000," with a sidecar and a sergeant-chauffer, in order to perform the duties of a liaison officer between the division and the squadron.

The first time I used my death-dealing friend at night was near the small locality of Stubno close to Yaroslav. Our target was a German unit protected by a machine gun, which maintained constant fire on us. I do not want to claim that my shots caused the Germans to retreat, but my marksmanship remains good even today, and I also think that at that time I put my powder together with the powder of my fellow soldiers with such a good result that we silenced our adversary and we had peace and quiet to sleep, for the time being at least.

The second time my friend-defender served me well was in the city of Sadova Vishnia, between Przemysl and Lvov, when we destroyed the strong rear guard of a German mountain infantry division which had entered Poland from Slovakia. One day later, however, my motorcycle was destroyed by German bullets, the chauffer wounded and I, in spite of a wound in my knee, had to "organize" a horse and continue my liaison duty as a cavalryman.

My rifle was not idle when near Yanov we defended the fords through the marshes for a long time against the superior weapons of our adversaries and abandoned our watery positions only when the Germans encircled us and used their bombers and strafing planes to disperse us. We crossed the Yanov forests, fighting our way toward Bzhuch near Lvov.

The master performance of my rifle-friend was in that very city of Bzhuch. Our defenses, despite lacking perfect organization, were nevertheless strong, for we held the western suburbs from early morning until late evening against German armour. Disregarding the fact that their tanks shot their way through our lines, destroying and burning all the nearby buildings, we prevented the German infantry from entering the city. I realized then that I had not cared for my rifle sufficiently. Due to constant firing she became so hot that I was unable to touch her metallic parts.

MAUSER 98

In the evening we received orders to fight through to Lvov. Too fatigued to start at once, we found shelter to spend the night. In the morning I became separated from Zbig, my school friend with whom I had passed all the campaign, and lost my horse, only to find another a few hours later. Not knowing the way to the city, I was particularly happy to enter it the next morning, and I was not alone, for I brought two Polish officers there with me.

According to later studies and statistics in regard to the September campaign, it is evident that from among three Polish divisions, the 11th, 24th, and 38th, only about eighty soldiers were able to reach Lvov. It is superflous to add that the territory between Bzhuch and Lvov was in German hands, but it was ironic to learn that among the German divisions was the famous mountain infantry whose rear guard was destroyed by us earlier at Sadova Vishnia.

I used several weapons during the war, among them a German Schmeisser that fell to me as booty. But they didn't last long. The Schmeisser was stolen; a carbine went with the horse which ran away in the forest; and a smallish-looking submachine gun I gave to a lieutenant-colonel in Lvov because he had no decent weapon for making his way to Hungary. Through all that time I kept my Mauser 98. Now that I was in the city I tried to repay my debt of gratitude to her, hoping that the care I was giving her would not be forgotten and that she would be to me as always, an unfailing friend in need. I was certain that she had no complaints whatsoever, for we remained true friends. Real friends for life and death but more for death, because she spewed death. I told her when and where. We were inseparable even in sleep—like an exemplary loving couple. When I slept, she was always in my arms.

The capitulation of the "City of Lions" (Lvov) to the Bolsheviks had shaken my Mauser and me. I seemed to hear her ask: "Why don't you use me? I was always true to you!" I had no answer.

The next day she was taken from me by the Red militiamen. The entry in my diary read: ". . .I don't have my rifle anymore and I am ashamed that I cried because of her loss, but it is not the end . . . despite the fact that it looks as if Poland is no more . . . and now it is up to me and others like me as to whether our country will exist again . . . It MUST arise again! Long live Poland!"

I changed to civilian attire and returned home.

The next day I joined a conspiratorial organization which consisted of my school friends. A few evenings later, a man came to see me whom I knew well but didn't like, because I thought him a coward. This time he gave me proof of his cowardice. He implored me to dispose of a very dangerous weapon which he had brought with him. I took it in my hands: A Mauser 98—and I read the familiar number of the barrel: 169921!

He left in a hurry as if afraid that I might change my mind. I remained standing in the middle of the floor, the rifle in my hands, smiling. . .

THE FIRST DAY WITH THE RUSSIANS

My brother jarred me awake. With eyes full of sleep I listened as he announced that a woman urgently wanted to see me. Noting the anxiety on his face, I dressed hurriedly. Out in the hall a young, good-looking, well-dressed young woman was sitting in a chair. *Well, I thought, the day is starting in a "good-looking" way.*

"Good-day," I greeted her. "What can I do for you?"

"You don't know me, but I do know you very well indeed, and I trust you completely. Please, trust me, too."

I was taken aback at her words. I had never seen her before and the longer she spoke, the more astonished I became.

"I am the servant in the villa of General "X," who has left with his family for Rumania. The house is full of valuables and no instructions have come to me as to their disposal. There are also arms, ammunition, and many military objects which worry me very much now that the Bolsheviks are coming. What should I do? I am at my wits end. Please, help me!"

Quick thinking was natural to me now.

"Go back home," I told her, "and pile all the things you want to get rid of in a room near the entrance. I shall be at your place in less than an hour. Hurry!"

She left and in five minutes I was ready to go too. Stopping at the homes of three of my good friends, I picked them up one by one and within thirty minutes we entered an elegant house in the finest section of the city.

Heck, I reflected, *those generals. They not only have the best looking houses but also the best looking maids!* But I was not really interested in this pretty girl, who considered me a miracle-worker. She stood at the door in front of me, looking at me gratefully with an inviting smile. I smiled back and quickly turned my head away. I was blushing up to my ears. I turned to my friends:

"Where shall we put all this stuff?" pointing to a pile of rifles, carbines, shotguns, hand guns, ammunition boxes, sabers, daggers, ornamental bayonets, and hundreds of other objects of military use, like map cases, binoculars, attaché cases, portfolios—all army issue, of the best quality, clean and shining.

"There is more to come," said the girl, "but I cannot handle it all by myself...unless you help me," and she smiled again. It was the same enigmatic smile, half coy, half challenging; bashful and half immodest—a smile in which I saw everything: sweetness, invitation, modesty, deviltry, virtue, sensuousness, innocence and desire. I wished I were a truck driver! I tore myself away from her uncanny gaze.

"Let's go! We should divide it all. Take home what you like; I will take the rest. Let's hurry!"

"How are we going to transport all that? Certainly not in our hands and not openly through the streets!" said one of the crew.

"Rudolf Gorski has a taxicab," I answered. "I saw him driving home. Joe!" I turned to him, for he knew Rudi very well. "Can you get Rudi and bring him here right away?"

"Sure, of course! If he's home!"

"If not, find him! You know how urgent it is! Get going!"

As he went out I addressed the girl, who had taken in the whole conversation. I knew she was willing to help.

"Do you have any military clothing, uniforms, blankets, that you want to get rid of?"

"Yes, naturally. The upstairs rooms are full of them. I was about to ask you to take them away too. What shall I do with the silver? There are full services of it and pitchers, cups, plates, and platters. I am afraid to keep it, for the Russians might think that I am a "capitalist lackey".

"Where are you from? Where do your parents live? Do you want to go home or remain here?" I questionned her.

She named a small city not too far from Przemysl and told me that she would prefer to go to her parents.

"Fine," I said, "you must take all the valuables with you and be responsible for them, but do not hesitate to sell anything or everything if you should be in need. Now, you have to help us wrap the arms in the military clothing and blankets or anything else and we will help you to do the same with all, I repeat, all the valuables. Then we have to find transportation for you. O.K?"

She agreed and we started to pack. We hurried up and downstairs piling in a corner near the main entrance door all the silver, crystal, expensive ornaments and everything that was of higher value according to our judgment. We worked silently and efficiently. The two piles, one ours, the other hers, grew higher and higher. We found a whole collection of military maps from the 1920 campaign which described the Polish counterthrust launched from the Bug River line against Marshall Tukhatchevsky's Red army, and many other interesting collections of historical and military maps. There were many books about military science, some confidential and classified materials concerning the findings of Polish intelligence with reference to Germany and Russia; the newest weaponry all around the world, with detailed descriptions, explanations, and annotations.

"We will have to study a lot," I told my friends. They agreed eagerly. We finished packing and waited for Joe and Rudi. We sat down, the girl, without being asked, brought each of us a large glass of wine. We accepted it with gratitude. Thirsty after having worked so fast and efficiently, we sipped and talked.

"The underground movement is the only salvation for us and for the nation," said Jack, the oldest of us, who attended a medical college. "Now we have enough weapons to arm a platoon. We must study military science, as Robert remarked before, and we are not alone. Every young man and woman will participate in doing the finest work possible. We have not perished yet!" he ended by paraphrasing the words of the Polish national anthem.

"Let's turn against the Germans, for they are the ones who started the war and destroyed our armed forces. Let's be clean in that which concerns the Soviets. Is that acceptable?" was my question. They answered in the affirmative.

"Where do I come in?" asked the girl. We looked at her in astonishment and saw that she was blushing—her lovely cheeks a deep crimson. Both her volunteering and her blushes made me feel excessively good.

"Your hometown is near the border and we will contact you soon at home. Until then you are supposed to keep everything secret. Do not forget that by talking to someone you could endanger the whole organization which we are about to set up and that you might thus endanger your very life and those of your parents and brothers and sisters."

"We have to have a leader, a recruiter, a planning unit, an executive detachment, a propaganda section, an instructional and educational chamber, a border group and a transportation outfit," I continued, "and I see you, Jack, as a leader; you, John, are a fine bookworm who should lead the instruction and education; Joe would be the best for transportation which he likes so much, including his motorcycle. I would like to be responsible for planning and recruitment. Is that all right with all concerned?"

They agreed, except Jack, who wanted me to lead together with him. I consented on condition that we would have to contact each other at least once a day—a suggestion he accepted.

"Where do I come in?" Marie asked again.

"You will probably be at your best in the liaison service in connection with the border group, but please, do not do anything yet, because one of us will contact you directly at your home." She nodded eagerly. "I ask you all to bring into our group your very best friends, but you must trust them so that you would be willing to lay down your life for them and vice versa. I see for my part the participation of a professor of mine, Dr. Hirski. As a young boy he participated in a 1917-18 Polish military conspiracy. I know him and vouch for him!"

"He is an excellent bet," agreed Jack and John.

"Let's meet tonight at my place. I have a nice room all to myself. Will seven P.M. be all right?" I asked. Everyone agreed.

"Here they come!" exclaimed John. "Joe, Rudi and Mitch!" Mitch was Joe's best friend and we all knew him well.

They entered without knocking and in a few minutes all the military objects were packed away in the car. We decided to take them all to my place. It was secluded and it would be easy for everyone to take away what he wanted. Marie had to wait until we came back to help her load her stuff.

The operation went smoothly. The taxi parked inside our garden in front of the large woodshed and we unloaded the contents in a few minutes. Returning to the villa and loading Marie's newly acquired "dowry" took us a little longer. Many pieces were breakable and we had to exercise the utmost care in order not to damage them.

"Jack, can you ride with Marie?" I asked him. He blushed and we all laughed. Marie's cheeks flushed with anger as she accused us of being cruel. We continued to laugh but stopped abruptly. She started to cry. She looked in vain for a handkerchief in her purse. Fortunately, I had a clean one in my breast pocket and I gently dried the tears from her eyes. Only then did I fully realize how beautiful she was. The beauty of some women shows when they cry; of others when they smile; of still others when they make love or become angry or when they pray. Ahh—women...

Jack got in the front seat of the car next to Rudi, the driver. Marie sat in the back. The taxi started and soon disappeared in the city streets. The four of us went through the house again taking some little things we liked. Concentrating on the books on some fine looking glassed-in shelves, I took as many as I could carry in a large sack. My friends gave me a helping hand, stuffing their sacks full of the ones I wanted and we carried them all to my house.

Rudi and Jack returned in an hour or so, and we repeated the book carrying, from the villa, which we cleaned out and also from the military library of the army corps command. After the book operation we drove to the houses left unattended by other generals and higher ranking officers who went abroad, repeating the pattern already established at Marie's house, or rather at the general's house where she was a maid. Some of the homes were left all to themselves, completely unattended. In others we met either domestics or distant relatives of the owners and we urged them to take the valuables while we were primarily interested in arms, ammunition and military objects. Our large shed soon filled up and I had to open another, my aunt's, who was out of town. By evening we had covered at least two dozen houses working at fever pitch. We had learned that the Soviet troops were occupying the barracks, police headquarters, city hall, post office, etc.

Rudi's friend, another taxi owner, assisted us with his car throughout the whole afternoon. We didn't have time to eat a regular meal, but there were plenty of sandwiches and coffee ready and waiting for us at our homes, so we ate them on the run and continued working. After my aunt's shed was filled we used two garages, Rudi's and Bol's. There was no one to stop us. The Polish police were hiding from the Soviets or had gone west with the Germans, together with their families and belongings. The Soviet militia was not yet functioning. It was only toward evening that we saw some men with rifles and red armbands walking the streets with rather timid and uncertain steps. They saw us in the cabs, but at the sight of seven young men riding in two taxis they didn't ask any questions. They were not quite sure of themselves yet, and, in addition, we knew them all and they knew some of us. We also noted that the government food storage warehouses were left open to the public the whole day, and there was no family that didn't take advantage of that fact. People were carrying home everything imaginable, by hand, in bags, sacks, suitcases, wheeling baby carriages, carts, using horse-drawn vehicles, and even in wheelbarrows. No one stopped them, for everyone knew well that each man had the right to live.

THE FIRST DAY WITH THE RUSSIANS

As it grew dark we heard some scattered shots. We decided to go home, knowing that we would meet at seven at my place. There was not too much time left before the time of our meeting. I tried to relax, but in vain. The activities of the day were too exciting to be dismissed in peace. My mother, upon hearing that friends were coming to our home, decided to go to church and then to visit some friends, so I knew that we would not be disturbed Just as she was leaving, there was a knock at the door.

Hm, I thought, *somebody is coming early,* and hurried to the door to open it.

"Marie!" I exclaimed. "What are you doing here?"

She was the last person I expected to see, the more so because it was only six-thirty.

"Everything is fine back home in Krasich. My parents were very glad to see me, and you should have been there at the moment of my arrival! Their eyes grew bigger at every item I unpacked and finally they became speechless at the sight of all the riches I brought home. As I left they were stashing everything away." She finished with a lovely smile.

As she talked I observed her. She looked just beautiful! Her dress was not showy, but tasteful, and its color together with that of her light overcoat, scarf, shoes and stockings, presented a delightful unity. Her speech was exquisite and so precise that I was unable to discern any regional accent whatsoever. *Interesting,* I reflected, *she does not speak like a maid.* I introduced her to my mother, who made some polite small talk and left us, smiling.

"Do you have a place to stay tonight?" I asked Marie.

"Yes, yes, I have many friends in the city."

"Wouldn't you prefer to stay with us? The meeting might exceed the curfew time."

"Well, we shall see. But don't put yourself to any trouble." She blushed and I did the same.

"Where did you go to school?" I changed the topic of conversation to cover up my embarrassment. "In Krasich?"

"Yes. There and here also. Last June I graduated with distinction from the State Teachers' College in Przemysl, but being unable to find a position in the educational field I took what was available—a maid's job."

"How did you like it? And did the general like you?"

"Please, don't make fun of me! Yes, he liked me so much that he even made some advances—in the most gentlemanly and polite way, but, nevertheless, they were clearly advances."

"Ha, ha, ha."

"There was nothing 'ha, ha, ha' about it. He was very nice and sweet and he knew how to take my 'no' for an answer."

"Say, Marie—do you remember what your first words were when you saw me today for the first time? You said that you knew me and my name, too. Please do not be offended when I say that your lovely person escapes my faulty memory . . ."

"Oh, so that's it! Well, I knew you because you were the actor and I was only a spectator together with hundreds of others, who would not be noticed by an actor."

THE FIRST DAY WITH THE RUSSIANS

"Me? An actor? I never played any role in a the-ater! You must be mistaken; it must have been some-body else!"

"Not at all! Maybe I used the wrong word, but it still holds. You were playing soccer and I attended all the games. My friend's fiance played on your team."

"Oh, that's why you considered me an actor! Did I really behave like an actor on the soccer field?"

"Yes, you did indeed. You always assumed the posture of a man who cared how he looked to the public. Do you remember the last game you played against Cra-covia which was lost by our team 5:1? And have you forgotten the fatal nail in your shoe which inflicted a wound in your heel? You see, we knew all that, because we carefully followed the progress of our team. Yours was a fine team, for you had won the championship of south-western Poland . . . It is a pity that we don't have much more time for conversation, because our friends will be arriving here any moment, but all my younger girl friends knew you and your colleagues and friends, and we used to talk a lot about your school, your teachers, and everyone in general. Przemysl is a relatively small city and everybody knew everybody else. Well . . ."

She didn't get a chance to finish the next sentence. I kissed her, gently at first and then I began to press her more firmly to me and to enclose her more strongly in my arms. She went limp and I was sure that she would have fallen, if she had not been seated in the deep chair. I pulled away from her after a long, long kiss.

There was a knock at the door and I looked at my watch. It was five minutes before seven. Marie turned her head toward the door and said too firmly:

"Come in!" It was Joe. Shortly afterward the others arrived. We all sat and talked until Jack took the floor.

"Friends," he said, "night is the friend of conspiracy. During the day we will not know each other. Our first day with the Russians has ended and now comes our first night—really ours! I take command of this group. I demand of you an unlimited trust, not only in me, but especially in the righteousness of our cause of freedom, practical Christianity, brotherhood and social justice! Thus, you see I have modified the tenets of the French revolution," he chuckled disarmingly. Then became serious again. "I demand complete mutual trust that cannot be broken by anyone, under any circumstances, at any time. May God Almighty help us in our decision to love the good, to combat the evil, to fight for the freedom of Poland, no matter at what cost, and for the freedom of all people— 'for your freedom and ours'—as it was written in the hearts of all Polish freedom lovers who have given their lives to this cause throughout Polish history. I open this our first meeting in the name of the Most Illustrious Polish Republic!"

Thus started the conspiracy.

God help us all!

CONCLUSION

There is no conclusion. There will be none as long as men are capable of fighting for "liberty and justice for all," the ideal older than Christianity and the timeless credo of mankind defended at the cost of the highest personal and national sacrifices in blood and at the cost of life itself.

The price of liberty is high—higher than life, which cannot be evaluated in materialistic terms as it defies any price put on it. Only the weak and characterless are willing to "make a deal" with evil. Their philosophy of not resisting evil is comparable to passive moral prostitution.

In the history of mankind, the Polish nation has always stood in the forefront as a champion of liberty among nations. Not a single battle has been waged in the name of freedom where Polish names were lacking. The bones of Polish freedom fighters strewn over all seven continents have not fallen there in vain. Countless volunteers have appeared as if out of nowhere for every fallen hero, and the struggle for man's highest values has ever continued afresh.

It was William Faulkner who repeated the key words of his great Polish predecessor, Henryk Sienkiewicz, "to uplift men's hearts"—where every thought, word and deed of men leading to that purpose is a defiance of death—a denial of death.

Thus immortality can result from the actions of mortals—through affirmation of life.

"I am the resurrection and the life", said the greatest teacher of man. Another wrote: *"...and the Word was God,"* while a modest contemporary philosopher expressed the same concept in more tangible and simple language: *"The almighty force that moves the universe is Love,"* for only love can produce freedom and justice in a practical way.

Some men find fault with this reasoning. They are the weaklings who question the importance of an individual in society, and in their negation ask whether anything at all can be done by the individual to influence the direction of economic, political and social developments. The simple answer to their negativism is the affirmative "yes" where everything in life, but absolutely everything, depends *just* on the individual. It is *only* he who can influence the current of life by his affirmative actions. But he must possess knowledge and expertise and at the same time, he should be *for something* rather than *against something*. And here education written with a capital "E" comes into play, furthering not only knowledge, but that which is formed in the first place and surpasses all other values—human personality and character strong enough to wage the eternal struggle for liberty and justice for all.

The names of the great men and women who have participated in that unending contest are written with golden letters in the hearts of mankind never to be forgotten. It is our supreme duty to ourselves and to posterity to strive for perfection, no matter how small and limited that segment of life which is ours, because only through this action do we achieve full-fledged membership in the human race.